DEVILS, GHOSTS, AND WITCHES

Occult Folklore of the
Upper Ohio Valley

An Anthology by
George Swetnam

Design and Illustrations
Laurel Smith

McDonald/Swärd Publishing Co.
"Preservation Hill"
Box 104A, R.D. #3
Greensburg, PA 15601

Volume I

Library of Congress Catalog Card Number: 88-90519

ISBN 0-945437-03-X

Printed by South Greensburg Printing Co., Greensburg, PA

First Edition, limited

McDonald/Sward Publishing Co.

Back Cover:

Portrait in oil of George Swetnam, presented to him in 1972 by the *Pittsburgh Press*
at his retirement. It was painted by the multi-award winning artist, Nat Youngblood,
who was with the Press for 34 years (arriving three years after Swetnam) and became
the art director of that newspaper. Famous for his watercolors, this Evansville, Indiana
native has also done much to preserve "Pittsylvania Country," as seen in his paint-
ings of landscapes, architecture, folklore, and pioneer history of the region.

Contents

CHAPTER 1 — **Ghosts, Goblins, and Spirits**

CHAPTER 2 — **Devil Tales**

CHAPTER 3 — **Witches and Warlocks**

CHAPTER 4 — **Curses**

CHAPTER 5 — **Wonder Tales**

CHAPTER 6 — **Superstitions**

About the Author

Certainly no name is more nearly synonymous with western Pennsylvania history than that of George Swetnam. No one has contributed more in the way of enjoyable and informative history, with a broad, scholarly, and intimate knowledge of this region. Western Pennsylvania owes much to George Swetnam, whose life has centered around history, folklore, and drama.

He is a legend in his own time. Swetnam was born "on a blustery day" in a village near Cincinnati, Ohio, the youngest of four children of William Wylie Swetnam, a mountain Kentucky school teacher and principal, and Flora May Stafford Swetnam, a well-known author at the turn-of-the-century. In his own words, "My parents were from Kentucky and before I could master a yankee accent they took me back to Kentucky." After free-lancing for literary, technical, and historical journals while in high school, Swetnam went on to graduate from the University of Mississippi, following attendance at the Universities of South Carolina and Alabama.

Turning to theology, the author graduated from Columbia Theological Seminary, with a degree of Bachelor of Divinity. Top honors in Hebrew (highest grades in school's 100-year history) led him to archeology and Semitic languages. He achieved a Master of Theology degree at Auburn (now Union) Theological Seminary and a Doctor of Philosophy degree in Assyriology at Hartford Seminary Foundation in 1930. He was the youngest student in America to win a doctorate in this most difficult field, where he deciphered 100 Sumerian clay tablets for his dissertation. At the University of Alabama, Swetnam taught English and German.

The author later operated a photo studio, worked with Victor Kepler and was staff cameraman for the Alabama football team, covering the 1935 Rose Bowl Game. Surprisingly enough, with all this behind him, George Swetnam traded his camera shop for a car and then became a hobo for two years, at times riding the rails in boxcars along with fellow adventurers, and at one time joined a group of itinerant fruit pickers — all experiences that greatly expanded his writing career.

George Swetnam eventually wended his way to Uniontown, PA. where he worked on the *Evening Standard* newspaper as staff writer and managing editor, before coming to Pittsburgh as feature writer for the *Pittsburgh Press* in 1943, continuing on for 30 years. It was during these years that he and his wife, Ruth, raised their three children, George, Anne, and John. For the Press he served as reporter, staff writer (re-write), and assistant magazine editor. Besides his own name he wrote under the pen names: Acker Petit, Francine Avery, B. Duke, Duke Barton, and Frank Mantews.

Swetnam, affectionately called "Swet" early in his career, wrote a plethora of articles on history and folklore and had his own "Press-time" column in the Sunday *Family Magazine* of that journal. Besides his many historical and folklore articles and lectures, he achieved immediate recognition for *Pittsylvania Country,* a volume in the distinguished "American Folkways" series.

The author was instrumental in forming the "Institute of Pennsylvania Rural Life and Culture" near Lancaster, PA. He was also editor of the *Keystone Folklore Quarterly* from 1959-65; was a speaker for six years for the Rose Hill Seminars; and currently serves on the advisory board for Sherwood Forest

Theater, since 1977. As an ordained Presbyterian minister, he continues to conduct church services and performs marriage ceremonies. He and his wife also host annual "Bob Schmertz" folksings.

In 1954 he was awarded the Lawrence S. Mayers National Peace Award which he received from Vice-President Nixon at the White House.

Some of his book titles include: *The Song of Deborah; Temple Archives, 2000 B.C.; Little Giant; The Singin' Family; The Bicentennial History of Pittsburgh and Allegheny County; So Stand Throughout the Years; Where Else But Pittsburgh; Star in the West; Heroes of the Cross; Pennsylvania Transportation;* (and in colaboration with Helene Smith) *Andrew Carnegie; Hannah's Town;* and *A Guidebook to Historic Western Pennsylvania,* as well as numerous plays. He and Smith headed Pittsburgh's Light Rail Transit historic survey, in addition to other historic surveys of the area. Swetnam has written a variety of industrial, medical, religious, and music histories.

But it has been said that "with almost as many letters after his name as there are in it, Swetnam has never paraded his honors, preferring to be judged by his work." In fact most people who know him are not aware of all of his erudition, for he never indicates doctor before or after his name.

In recent years the Executive Committee of the Pennsylvania Council for the Social Studies gave George Swetnam an official commendation and citation for his services to Pennsylvania history:

> Once, in your homey, humble way, you said to me, "This is all and this is me." But this is the George Swetnam we in the Pennsylvania Council for the Social Studies are willing, able, and proud to honor in commendation and recognition at Seven Springs this April 8, 1972, in a small corner of your Pittsylvania Country and where, in all our minds and hearts, you are our "Star of the West."

Foreword

Lest some ultraconservative scholars feel obliged to denounce much of this material as not being "real" folklore, I hasten to explain that it follows the principle enunciated forty years ago by that seminal scholar, Ben A. Botkin of the Library of Congress:

The essence of folklore . . . is something that cannot be contained in a definition but that grows upon one with folklore experience. Old songs, old stories, old sayings, old beliefs, customs, and practices — the mindskills and the handskills that have been handed down so long that they seem to have a life of their own, a life that cannot be destroyed by print but constantly has to get back to the spoken word and be renewed; patterned by common experience; varied by individual repetition, inventive or forgetful; and cherished because somehow characteristic or expressive; all this, for want of a better word, is folklore.

Botkin, B.A., *A Treasury of American Folklore, etc.,*
New York, 1944

A Word to the Reader

Ghost stories and their cousins — tales of witches, devils, curses and wondrous events — are for fun, for reading, recalling and telling, best when the light is dim and the fire burns low, and the grisly wind howls or whines, and clouds gather to promise (or threaten, according to our mood) the glare of lightning and the roar of thunder to follow.

Man is both a timorous and an inquisitive creature, drawn by nature to approach as close as safety seems to warrant, and seek, albeit fearfully, that which is beyond our ken; to come as near as we can to the fire, hopeful of not being burned. Although we try to hide and refuse to admit it, the belief in witchcraft, superstitions and supernatural phenomena is, as my departed friend, Patrick Gainer, once wrote, universal and ancient. It is not confined to the mountain and foothills. We city folk have our taboos and folklore as well. We may laugh as we cross our fingers or knock wood, but it is a nervous just as much as it is a concealing laughter. When we speak of "the deceased," or someone as "gone away" (or, at the opposite end of the scale, "kicked the bucket" or "cashed in his checks") we are tacitly admitting our fear of saying "death" lest the very word should strike us. And note how few will say the word "cancer," but beat about the bush and perhaps say "malignant." And consider the recent rash of newspaper want-ads offering thanks to some saint and asserting that for others, if they will promise to do the same in print, wishes are certain to be granted.

This material is a selection from what has been collected during a forty year study of the indigenous folklore of the Upper Ohio Valley, both oral and from printed sources over many years, which has proved much too voluminous for even a fair sampling of all the branches to be printed in one volume. Perhaps other segments may be forthcoming in future years.

Some critics who still look on folklore as most of us once did, as "the literature of the illiterate," may object to the inclusion of material from books, newspapers and other such sources; we must face the fact that type does not change the nature of the thing printed — truly a real superstition. Some of these stories have been previously printed in the *Keystone Folklore Quarterly, West Virginia Folklore,* (which the late Ruth Ann Musick of Fairmont State College published for years as a labor of love), and the *Pittsburgh Press,* during the time when I worked there. These last (since I was paid to do them) by permission of John Troan when he was editor. Some are from early histories (yes, folklore gets into histories, too), autobiographies and other books, and from early newspapers.

Ghost stories, like other folklore, are of many types, conditioned by the thinking of those among whom they grew and were passed along, the scenes or people or events with which they were originally connected. Unusual houses or natural places have their ghost tales, as do mines, mills, bridges and mountains. My own home near Pittsburgh is said to have two ghosts, one its builder, an important railroad man at the turn of the century, the other perhaps a servant girl, a gentle poltergeist. Some persons report having had strange experiences here. But most ghost tales are true folklore, so close to people's thinking and emotion that they feel free to pass them along as their own experiences, without any feeling of falsehood. While many city folk today are hesitant about expressing any belief in ghosts, others, under favorable conditions, will relate such experiences as freely as the tales I heard in my boyhood in the mountains of Kentucky, of ghosts seen by my grandfather and an uncle. Even more admit a belief in presentiments or ''second sight.''

Without question, ghost tales are less frequent today than in the years before similar thrills could be provided by radio or television, or the horror films now available. But when someone breaks the ice in a small group today, perhaps in dusk or storm, or by firelight, others will often chime in and bell like answering bucks in a forest.

Tales involving witches are, and apparently have always been less frequent in the Upper Ohio Valley than ghost stories, despite the fact that more people of the area actually believe in necromancy than in departed spirits. Public response after I had reported the existence of some persons professing to be practicing witches and warlocks would lead me to believe that almost a fourth of people in this area actually believe in witchcraft.

For some obscure reason, devil tales have never been so common in the area as ghost tales, in view of the fact that while only a minority of people of this area would admit belief in ghosts, even fewer would seriously deny a belief in His Satanic Majesty.

Few examples of superstitions and similar folk beliefs are included here, and these are instances of their recognition as such, because such taboos and practices are still so common as not to need specification.

The purposes of this book are two-fold: Principally for the enjoyment of the reader, and partly as glimpses of the thinking and life of the people of this area during its more than two hundred years of European based culture. For this reason I have not thought it worthwhile or even wise to clutter the text with footnotes, except in rare instances and for reporting the sources, nor to add an appendix with information as to the motifs and types assigned by professional folklorists to the tales and legends. It is doubtful if two percent of the readers will be such students of folklore, and most of these would be able to make such assignments without my aid, and probably enjoy doing this for themselves.

Since this is an anthology, the spelling, punctuation, capitalization, and style are inconsistent. It all varies, depending upon the author of each section and the period of time in which each was written.

The area included in this study is the Ohio Valley and its tributaries from above the mouth of Big Sandy River.

— George Swetnam, Pittsburgh, 1988

There is nothing impossible in the existence of the super-natural; its existence seems to me decidedly probable.
— *George Santayana*

1

Ghosts, Goblins, and Spirits

Ghosts were created when the first man woke in the night.
                                    — *James Matthew Barrie*

Ghost tales and similar stories come in all shapes and sizes; moods varying from the depressive and frightening to the sentimental and sweet, and on a wide variety of subjects, from the historical — often associated with the names of famous persons (real or imaginary), or impressive and mysterious houses, to places associated with tragic and often criminal events. They may be concerned with people, places, and things of the long past, or fairly recent happenings.

An example of the historical occult about real persons is *"Angel or Dog?"* concerned with the Rev. George Scott, an early preacher and missionary to the frontier, and John Murrell (cq), the late robber-murderer of the Natchez Trace. One involving an imaginary character is *"Joe Magarac"* though that was not the early name of this character born of the needs of oppressed and friendless Slavic immigrants.

Houses, especially taverns, stimulated ghost tales in part because of the millennia-old theme of the murderous innkeeper (Procrustes of the ancient Greeks, Colonel Plug in *"Angel or Dog?"*). An example is *"Yank Brown's Deathbed."* Places where deaths had occurred are another fruitful source, such as *"Who Will Take Me Home?"* and especially if crime was involved, as in *"The Missing Knife."* In fact, almost anything exciting the imagination seems to have tended to breed stories of ghosts, goblins, and spirits. *"The Man From Hogback"* is a typical goblin narrative.

Here are a few of the many stories of this type to be found in the Pittsylvania Country.[1]

---

[1] In 1759 a group of people passed a resolution requesting that the Crown set up a fourteenth colony at the headwaters of the Ohio River to be called "Pittsylvania." Although the colony never materialized, the term has ever after been associated with the region.

The Ghost in The Abbey

Ghosts have often walked in the Pittsylvania Country, to judge by the number of stories of such activity in the past. Even today, when it has become unfashionable to believe in them, there are still occasional reports.

Oddly enough, one of the least frequently remembered here is the best attested on record in this area. It is the story of a Benedictine monk, whose spirit appeared daily in St. Vincent's Abbey at Latrobe in the late fall of 1859.

The account is not merely a matter of history, but was officially vouched for at the time by Abbot (later Archabbot) Boniface Wimmer, founder and for many years head of the community.

Its first notice in print appears to have been an item in the Pittsburgh Dispatch of Feb. 20, 1860, written in the antiquated style of journalism in that day. It ran:

A QUEER STORY — A report is current in some circles in the two cities [Pittsburgh and Allegheny] — we don't know on what founded — that recently, while Mass was being celebrated at Latrobe, the spirit of some priest or saint appeared, and communicated the information to the assembly that it was all a misapprehension about Purgatory, no such intermediate state of probation existing, and worse than all, that but two priests had yet found their way to Heaven. We don't know what could have originated the story, but it is positively current, and we mention the matter to learn how it got afloat. Can anybody give us the origin?

Like many rumors, the story was considerably garbled. But apparently someone gave a copy of the paper to Abbot Wimmer a little less than a week after publication. On Feb. 26 he sat down and wrote in the "Editors, Dispatch," a full and accurate account of the matter, which was published on March 1, apparently with his approval. At least, there is no indication of his objecting to such use.

Now in assessing what he had to say, it is only fair to consider Abbot Wimmer as a man and as priest. If he were ignorant, sick, or in his dotage, his statement might be lightly brushed aside. Far from that, however, he was well educated, physically and mentally strong, and in the prime of life — barely 51, and with more than 25 years of activity ahead of him.

Born in Bavaria on Jan. 14, 1809, Boniface Wimmer entered the University of Munich in 1827 to study law, but switched to theology, and was ordained as a priest in 1831.

For the next 15 years he divided his time between parish ministry and teaching theology. And in 1846, with backing from the King, he started for America with four students of theology, and 15 lay brothers of various professions. On Oct. 24 of that year he laid the foundation of St. Vincent's.

It wasn't easy. They were half starved that winter. But he was a big man and a natural leader, and swung an axe with the best of them, felling trees to build log cabins. He also ministered to Catholics in Greensburg, Saltsburg, and Indiana, for clergymen of his faith were scarce in Western Pennsylvania in that day. The next year Dr. Peter Lechner and 20 others joined them.

Things went well. Late in 1854 he was called to Rome, and in 1855 was made abbot for a period of three years, and apparently to serve after that until replaced. Returning to America, he journeyed in 1856 to the frontier areas of Minnesota and Kansas, where he planted communities of Benedictines, one of which became an abbey in 1866, the other 10 years later.

Abbot Wimmer continued active for a long time. He spent 1876-77 planting communities in Louisiana, North Carolina, Alabama, and Georgia. And in 1881 he was busy at the same work in Illinois.

By 1882 he was in charge of eight priories, 17 parishes, and 14 missions, with 150 orders, 116 lay brothers, and 85 scholastics.

In all, since coming to America, he had founded three abbeys, 12 priories, 45 parishes, 43 missions, and had trained 151 priests, 60 clerics, 19 novices, 177 lay brothers, and 150 scholastics. He had founded six colleges and ministered to 42,000 parishioners. In 1883 he was made archabbot, and died in 1887.

Here is what this man, in mid-career, and speaking exactly to correct an error, had to say about the ghost:

> A friend of mine handed me a copy of the Dispatch, of the 20th instance, drawing my attention to a "Queer Story" telling that recently, while "Mass" was being celebrated in Latrobe, the spirit of some priest or saint appeared and communicated the information to the Assembly that it was all a misapprehension about "purgatory," no such state of probation existing, and worse than all that, but two Priests had found their way to Heaven.
>
> The truth is that at St. Vincent Abbey near Latrobe, a Novice saw from the 18th of September until the 19th of November, 1859, every day from eleven to twelve o'clock a.m. or from twelve to two o'clock in the night, the apparition of a Benedictine Monk in his fall festival dress. After all he asked in the presence of another member of the order, what he wanted. The spirit then answered that he had been suffering seventy seven years already, because he had not said seven Masses of obligation; that he had appeared to seven other Benedictines at different times and had not been heard; and that he would have to appear after eleven years again if he would not help him. He wanted the seven "Masses" said for him, besides this, the Novice should, for seven days, observe the strictest silence and retreat and more, he

3

should say for thirty three days, each day three times, the "Fiftieth Psalm," barefooted and his arms stretched out.

This was done from the 21st of November til the 25th of December, when the last Mass was celebrated and the Ghost disappeared. During this time he appeared several times exhorting the Novice most impressively to pray for the Souls in Purgatory, since they suffer very hard, and consequently are very thankful for those who concur to their redemption; and sad enough, said that of the five Priests who had already died at the Abbey, not one was yet in Heaven, but suffering in Purgatory.

This is the substance the facts that gave origin to the strange report. We give it that much credit as it deserves, but this report is correct.

The meaning of his final paragraph appears to be that he vouched for the fact that the ghost had appeared as reported, but may have had some reservation in mind as to whether it was actually the spirit of a Benedictine monk, and as to whether what it said was true.

It has often been a matter of remark how many such apparitions are reported to have been priests who were derelict in their duties. Some students of such matters have taken the position that such wandering spirits are driven by their own guilt feelings, rather than any divine punishment; and it is not unlikely that the most deeply conscientious would be greatly concerned over comparatively small faults.

On the other hand, many who attribute such apparitions to evil spirits, point out that the Devil can give himself and his emissaries any form he chooses, and which will fit his own purposes.

One thing is certain; that Abbot Wimmer was fully convinced that the apparition, whether true or false, had been seen daily at the abbey for more than three months. And his failure to name the person mentioned as "another member of the order" may be simply his modest way of saying that when appealed to by the frightened novice, he himself braved the presence of the apparition, so as to give the younger man courage to speak.

It appears certain that while he may have doubted the words of the spirit, he at least agreed to the novice's carrying out its request.

However these things may be, the matter created a considerable stir, so much so that later a member of the order, one Paul Keck, charged Abbot Wimmer with favoring and promoting spiritualism rather than the Catholic faith.

So seriously was the charge regarded that the abbot was summoned to Rome in 1865. But after the whole matter had been examined, he was not only upheld, but in July 1866 was confirmed permanently as abbot, and in 1869, was named as a member of the Vatican Council.

From contemporary statements of those who were in position to know the facts, it would appear that Keck was ejected from the order, although I have not been able to confirm this absolutely.*

*   *   *   *   *   *   *

*In the **Latrobe Bulletin** (June 25, 1976) Barbara H. Nakles in a special article for the newspaper revealed the following, under the heading, "Area Had Share of 'Eerie Events' ":*

One of the most famous area ghosts was that of a priest who walked more than 100 years ago in the St. Vincent Church. George Swetnam of Pittsburgh wrote the story of this apparition . . . According to Swetnam, a spirit of "a benedictine Monk in his fall festival dress" appeared to a Novice, asking him for prayers and masses to be said. When these were performed, the ghost was not seen again in the church.

However, Richard Burkholder of Latrobe is not certain that the priestly figure disappeared for good. He tells a story of an encounter with an unearthly figure which took place one summer evening in 1936.

At that time, Burkholder worked at the St. Xavier farm. After visiting in Hostetter, he and a friend, John Bialon, were walking back to the academy. Bialon was killed a few years later in World War II.

The two young men went past the airport and walked along old Route 30. It was about 1:30 a.m. The moon was so bright, said Burkholder, that you could have seen a nickel on the ground 20 feet away.

After passing the airport, they stopped to rest. They were on a bridge which spanned a small stream. They decided to sit for a few minutes on the abutment.

Suddenly they heard a slight noise which appeared to come from the water below them.

"Did you say something?" asked Burkholder.

"No," came the answer.

Burkholder turned his head to look back along the road they had just travelled. There, standing 10 to 15 feet away, was a strange figure. The "thing" was over six feet tall.

"I'm sure that it was a man," said Burkholder, "even though I couldn't make out a face."

The ghost had no eyes yet the boys felt that it was staring at them. The face was gray and darker short hair stood up on top like a crew cut.

The figure was neither thin nor transparent. It was husky with very broad shoulders. No arms were visible. The apparition was draped in a long black gown which fell in folds to the ground. The robe was cinched by a wide belt which was darker and shinier than the gown.

John Bialon, by this time, also had turned to stare at the visitor. For a moment, the two were frozen. Then Burkholder said, "Let's get out of here."

5

* Swetnam, George, "The Ghost in the Abbey," *Pittsburgh Press,* April 7, 1968.

Both got up and began to walk toward St. Xavier's. The walk turned into a jog and then broke into a headlong run. They didn't stop until they ran out of breath. Only then did they dare to look behind them. Nothing was there.

At that time, Burkholder had never heard of the St. Vincent ghost. Years later when he heard that story, he felt that perhaps he had seen the same spirit. He says that the figure he saw appeared to be a priest. And, as he says, he didn't wait around to find out if it had a message for him.

Many other ghost stories have been told about locations in the area. A house in Cooperstown, another on Baker Hill, and Salem Church and cemetery all have been called haunted. White, floating figures, an organ playing in an unoccupied building, and strange sounds have been reported.

Whether or not you believe in ghosts, the strange happenings provide the basis for interesting stories.

The Graveyard Stand

Just back of Farmington where the widow Dean lives, on the old Braddock road below an old orchard and graveyard, was an old stand kept by Henry Beall and others 90 years ago. It was often called the graveyard stand, from the fact of a graveyard being close by. It was a large two-story log hotel, plastered and ceiled overhead with plank, and at that time was called the finest house on the old Braddock road. Some 60 years ago old Thomas Dean says he went to school in it to a preacher by the name of James Snyder. In the cellar in one corner the dirt looked like a grave, and it was thought by the scholars someone was buried there. After the school was out a family moved into it a short time and left, and people said it was haunted; something in white could be seen in the house and around it. It stood vacant for several years and was then torn down, and of late years some hearing of the old tales of this ghost, have fancied they could see something where the old tavern stood.*

Angel, or Dog?

This story is an example of the expansive and exaggerated style of Harry Moore, a newspaperman and folklorist of the region, more than sixty years ago. In recording the story of the Rev. George Scott, a very early preacher of southern Beaver County (PA), who made trips through the wilderness to carry the gospel to settlers and Indians alike, Moore inserts references to mythical and actual villians, and even invents words (such as ''threnardier,'' for ''murderer'') when it suits his fancy. Murrell (which Moore spells as Murrill) was

6

* S.T.W. (Samuel T. Wiley), ''Legends of Fayette County,'' *Genius of Liberty,* Uniontown, PA, September 28, 1881.

an actual highwayman, who sometimes posed as a spell-binding preacher, but so far as is known, never visited this area. We include only part of this long tale.

Upon an evening of a day memorable in his memory for self-communion, recast of duty and renewed devotion to his quest set out upon, [the Rev. George Scott] threaded a narrow gorge, infernally adaptable to the operations of one Jack Hare — its actual overlord.

An unaccountable light shone 'round, that as suddenly dissolved into an extremely comely yellowish-gray dog of size. Void of ostentation, or preamble whatever.

Not the least obeisance made he;
Nor a moment stopped or stayed he;

but immediately charged the gorge, as if certain of a lurking enemy, and equally assured of clearing the "Muscovite" out. Returning, the canine indulged in neither bark, wag of tail nor pantomime of his kind. Apparently masterless, yet masterful, sometimes he moved in front of pony and rider, sometimes he ambled behind; sometimes he suddenly toured the wood, as might a lion.

Arriving at next hostelry to halt for the night, it proved none other than that of Connelley type of a Threnardier.

As it was, as in a nightmare, that ever he lodged, stealthy footsteps falling like leaves or catlike, ever and anon, stole near and nearer his couch. Struggle as he might, he lay powerless to act, helpless save only to listen — unable to grapple the heard but unseen terror.

Rose the growl of a dog to discount that of a tiger — an intercepting growl — and one that retreated the threatening footfalls. Once, twice and again, as wore the night away, they came — the footfalls as before. And again the growl that daunted.

Dismissing the impression as fabric of a vision and unsubstantial, the preacher rose breakfasted and seeing the mysterious dog chained, felt surer that any growl of his that night, and so near his bedside, was impossible — unthinkable. Thinking it also wrong to appear to appropriate property of another, he consigned the creature attaching himself to his expedition, to the Threnardier — who'd sadly mistaken the renowned Brady, for an easy mark — of whom Scott later knew, — and who Joseph-like might have interpreted the traveler's dream.

Noontide shadows were softly falling; obliquely athwart reveries of our energetic gospel zealot, pursuing his path, when suddenly as before, a light shone 'round; glowed an expanse and again the resolvent dog — sans bark — sans wag of tail and seemingly empowered with ubiquity.

Afternoon to follow wore rapidly away, bringing death to a super-mountain rattler about to fang the pony when dismembered by the alert and agile dog. Little apparently recked the preacher, only notic-

7

ing the close call to his faithful carriage and giving the freer rein to the docility; long selecting own trail and gait thereon.

In such a manner did the trio, preacher, pony and dog, arrive at the next stop or inn.

Per custom the pony drew attention of the rugged men about. No more so, now, than did the unusual dog. But, our Pilgrim-Exegist, only the more assiduously assisted mine host to secure the latter animal in a heavily puncheoned mule corral — chained down to secure beyond a doubt, his final detention. Up and early in the morning did our preacher ride away.

Noon at the hostel was put behind by this. High noon and mine host was hugging himself over the rare acquisition of the finest specimen of dog ever clapped eyes upon — when was heard the rending of a chain and clang —

as if a hundred anvils rang,

immediately followed by a crash through the vain puncheon slabs as they were pasteboard.

Lifting his hands and looking up, our Boniface [innkeeper] saw by the succession of the gray and yellow streaks, that the wayfaring dog knew which direction the holy man had taken.

Again, the incandescence of a bright and shining light, yielded to the preacher the caninity of a yesterday. Convinced, that the dog's owner now lived ahead the Rev. Dr. Scott made no further effort to balk the persistent animal's determination to pursue.

And now did hitherto preacher, pony and dog, as day succeeded halcyon day, plunge the deeper into one vast immensity, solitude, density profound and wilderness of wood. Earth blending with sky, were swallowed in immurement of forest. Rapter and holier sanctity imbued the day's march into which, apparently, had stolen angels. Long after our Exegist to name, declare the singularly omnipotent blessedness in which near heaven bent down; when was heard the rustling of pinions, and the very whisperings of an approving God.

A female panther glared from an arching limb; but, at a rush of the dauntless dog, quailed crouching to her lair. A monster bear, hunger-eyed, lunging aggressively on our trio's trail, retreated suddenly and precipitately whence he came. A snow-white dove circling the pony once, twice and thrice, settled for an instant on the head of the gracious dog. At which series of manifestations, the enthused pastor to be, overflowing with fervor of the Kingdom brought nigh, prayed for the fulfilment of promise made by the Church Militant. Prayed as never before, for his Transylvanian Diocese, Episcopate or Presbytery. Strongly and fervently his voice went up for those whose love had been his shield. Essaying to sing, the deep diapason of his psalm, mingled with the mystic music of the tossing pines.

Singing he rode, oblivious of doubt, dole or danger. Reins of the pony the while, lay loose upon its gentle neck, as thus he proceeded down the slope leading to where the Raccoon Creek unites with that of Service. Our preacher thus engaged, had just gathered up his bridled lines, — was just about to essay the swollen ford ahead, when a large, powerfully-built, determined-looking man, coming forward with a fierce oath, bade him desist his singing, dismount, say nothing and disgorge. He had scarcely spoken, when the dog upspringing, bore Murrill to earth with heavy impact. For Murrill it was.

Instantly dismounting, bidding the infuriated dog to desist, — very kindly and compassionately did the considerate Rev. George Scott raise J. B. Murrill to his feet; — Who with scant apology, at breath, brushed briskly into the abounding elders; casting behind such a look of terror as limners give the apostate disciple.

Turning to break silence of his hitherto, unappreciated, timely, four-footed friend, the further wildered divine saw that grayish-yellowishness vanish into the thin and haunted air as super-naturally as had been, its suggestive comings.

Awe-stricken, and self-reproachfully, the subdued pastor of the Mill Creek Congregation of then Cayuga County, Va., rode silently, slow and solemnly the few remaining miles of his errantry.

Rode them imbued with firm belief, that a manifested, especial providence had guarded his peculiar, danger-beset and noteful pilgrimage.

About the subsequent career of Murrill figuring at the ford, lingers a contrariety of record, varied, heroic as that of any knight of Teutonic Order or Arthur's Table Round — Detraction has drawn the black lines of heartlessness, murder of a drover, rapine in bad taste, but, never denying him his splendid conception of spoils to the needy; as said of one Caesar:

> When that the poor hath cried,
> Murrill hath wept.

Again we note, that the confessedly intentional robber, in his instance, asserts a Personage in White opposed him at the Fordings — that the Rev. Scott as positively states a dog determinedly following him for days, sprang at the bandit's throat.[1]

Summing up, — both narrators agree as to date, place and other detail and other evidence shown an ubiquitous dog, that neither chain could bind nor bolt restrain, had figured down to the wending streams.

To us it comes, — Did either preacher or hold-up man misstate what he was mystically (no doubt) given to see?*

The Millvale Apparition

Another outstanding instance of a ghost in a church was

[1] Dr. Scott kept a diary, of which apparently no trace has been seen in almost a century. I find no such incident in Murrell's alleged confession.

* Moore, Harry; *Early and Later Lore of the Ohio Valley* (privately printed, 1922), p. 21ff.

reported by Louis Adamic in a national magazine in 1938. It had occurred about four years earlier while the noted artist, Maximillian Vanka, was painting the famous murals in St. Nicholas Catholic Church in Millvale, a close-in Pittsburgh suburb. The report of which this is a part is in the words of Vanka; and Fr. Zagar, shortly before his death a few years ago, assured me the story was correct. The church is still closed and locked from dark till dawn except for necessary occasions.

On the fourth night, as I say, while mixing paint and feeling rather cold and tired but not exhausted, I glanced at the altar beneath me, which was rather fully illumined by my lamp's downward flood of light . . . and there was a figure, a man in black, moving this way and that way in front of it, raising his arms and making gestures in the air.

I thought of course that the man was Father Zagar and, in my frenzy of work, I did not take a very good look at him. I was slightly annoyed for a moment. He had agreed to stay out; now here he was! But then I said to myself I had no right really to require him to keep out.

*   *   *   *   *   *   *

Father Zagar came in shortly before eleven, unlocking and locking the door, and cracking his usual jokes, boasting he had sent the ghost packing — when the whole *komedia* started all over again. There was again that strange awful knock or click in one corner under the choir, then another in the other corner. "O-ho!" cried Zagar, scratching his head. I used up what paint I had in the pail, then laid everything aside and got off, intent on fleeing, for I was abruptly all cold inside and beginning to drip with perspiration. But the Father detained me, seizing my arms, suggesting we face the situation. "Not I," said I and made for the door, Zagar after me, seizing me again.

There was another knock, I couldn't tell just where, but it cut into me like a knife. Then I saw him — the old man in black — moving down the aisle altarward. Terrified, horror-stricken, panicky are faint words to describe my sensation. "Look, Father," I yelled, "there he goes — to the altar — he's at the altar — *he's blown out the light!*" The last few words I shrieked out with more lung power than I ever thought I possessed, and simultaneously lost sight of the figure and began to feel a trifle better.

This — his putting out the light — is perhaps the most important point in the story. The light was "the sanctuary lamp" which usually hangs in a special fixture depending from the ceiling above the altar. It burns all the time (the nuns next door see to it) and is for that reason called also *vjechno svjetlo,* eternal light. The tallow and wick inside the bulb need to be changed only about once a year; and the sisters assured us afterward that as long as any of them had been there — for eight years, at any rate — it had never been out. The glass bulb round the flame is so wrapped that it is almost impossible to blow it out. No wind or draft can touch it; besides, all the doors and windows were closed . . . The light usually hangs, as I say; but now, because of the scaffolding, the fixture had been pulled up and the lamp stood like a huge red cup on the altar, where the ghost, or whatever it was, now blew it out with a puff of breath.

When I yelled that he had put out the light, Father Zagar demanded, "What light?" I said, "The eternal light! Can't you see it's out?"

"Bome, by golly!" he exclaimed and rushed to the altar, where he saw that the wick in the lamp was still smoking. He touched the lamp; it was hot. The flame had, obviously, just been extinguished.

Meantime I had left the church. The dogs were yelping and squealing outside. Father Zagar followed me out. "Till now," he said, "I still had a glimmer of doubt. I thought possibly it was your fantasy. I thought possibly I had imagined the knocks in the church and by my bed the other night. But now I believe."*

"Who Will Take Me Home?"

The trip westward was filled with many dangers; not only with the Indians but also with the climbing of hills and the crossing of rivers. As with many pioneers, Bob Phillips found his trouble while camping in a valley. This wasn't an ordinary valley. This valley seemed peaceful and was just the place to hole up for the night. But Bob was soon to find out that this valley was the mysterious "valley of the lost."

Bob had heard of such a place, but this couldn't be it. This valley was calm and restful; not wild with the sounds of a child who was lost — maybe even dead.

Everything seemed restful until about 9:30 that night. Bob had tied his horse on its rope to graze and had finished washing his dishes in the cool stream when out of what seemed nowhere a child's scream echoed through the valley, a scream which was full of hate, full of loneliness, and full of sadness and death.

Instead of being like most people who ran from the valley, Bob looked for this child. But she was not to be found. He searched until morning, and then he did find three graves — one of a woman named Sara, a man named Tom and the last a child. But this stone had no name.

All at once, he heard a child crying, and then he saw a small girl of about five years old. But Bob could see through this child — could she be dead? She must be dead!

Yet, she cried, she walked, she asked, "Will you take me home?"

At first Bob was shocked, but then he asked, "Where is your daddy and mommy, dear?"

The little girl pointed to Bob and said, "Please help me find my mommy." Then she added, "I must go now." And before Bob could say another word, she was gone — she had just disappeared.

* Adamic, Louis, "The Millvale Apparition," *Harper's,* Vol. 176 (April 1938), pp. 479; 482-83.

Bob saddled his horse, and started to leave when the little girl reappeared and said, "Please don't leave me. Help me find my mommy."

Bob asked, "What is your mommy's name?"

"Here name is Sara," answered the small child.

Bob remembered that the name on the tombstone had said Sara. Could her mother be the same Sara, he thought? He also remembered then that a woman, her husband and small child were heading for a new home when a rock slide had covered their wagon killing all three of them. The rest of the traveling party had buried all of them but had only finished carving the names of the parents when the cries at night began. They became afraid and had left without finishing the child's stone.

With tears in her eyes she answered, "Alice Louise Barker. My daddy is Thomas Barker, and my mommy is Sara Barker. But I can't find them, and I have looked for so long."

Bob told the little girl to follow him, and he walked to the graves. He pointed to each grave and then began to tell the little child about heaven. He spoke, "Far away from here there is a place that is called heaven. This is a very special place where mommies and daddies meet their little children. When the rocks fell on your mommy and daddy and you, they decided to go to this place called heaven. You were supposed to go too. But in the confusion, I think you were accidentally separated from them. Your mommy and daddy are waiting for you in heaven. Do you want to go to them? If you do, all that you do is say this prayer with me. "Dear God, let me come home with Mommy and Daddy. Amen."

The small child repeated this prayer, and a very bright light shone on her grave. She smiled, and her face lit up and as she slowly disappeared, Bob heard her say, "Thank you for taking me home. Mommy is waiting for me." Then she was gone.

That night when Bob rested from the day's experiences, the cries of the child were not heard. She had gone home.*

The Belated Burial

Several years ago in a small community near what is today Grafton, West Virginia, there lived a man and a woman who had only one child. Mary Jane was their daughter's name. She was a sickly child from the time she was born. Her parents had such a devotion for Mary Jane that they had her preserved when she died at the age of ten. It was a miraculous feat which was performed by an undertaker. The undertaker had developed the method of preservation after

12

* Stanley, Penny, "The History and Legends of Prickett's Fort," *West Virginia Folklore* (Fairmont, WV: 1966) XVI, 3-4, pp. 12-13.

many long years of experimentation. The cost, however, was almost unbelievable. The parents agreed to pay a large sum of money down and to complete the balance of the payment over the next few years.

Mary Jane was enclosed in a casket which had a clear top so that her parents could look at her and be with her at all times.

For the first couple of years everything went along as had been planned. After a while, however, Mary Jane's father became ill and was unable to work. But in order to keep up with the payments, he borrowed money. After a while he went so far in debt that he couldn't borrow another penny. When he stopped making the payments, the undertaker came to their home and took the little girl's body from the house to his shop where he opened the glass and put her in a regular casket and buried her.

Naturally the parents were horrified at the thought, but due to financial conditions were unable to stop the undertaker and his greedy actions.

To this very day, however, the old folks say that on her birthday each year Mary Jane can be seen playing in the front yard of her home.*

The Pegleg Ghost

One half mile directly eastward from the village of Knoxville, and a few rods south of what was once the Pine Tree club house, can still be seen the ruins of a once modest red brick house which stood in a narrow swampy valley. This house for three score years had been shrouded in a haze of weird stories such as is borne by none other in the whole countryside. For this reason all these long years it has been known far and wide as the haunted house on Croxton's Run.

The first owner of these few acres, a man by the name of Cooper, was a greedy, unfriendly character. When he located on this virgin soil he built his farmhouse close to a cool, gushing spring of water as was the custom in pioneer days. This spring was the fountainhead and source of the uniquely named Sally Fisher Fork of Croxton Run, now a dirty little stream that meanders at the base of precipitous hills and flows into the Ohio on its northern flank. The name of this run is in honor of the lady who became the wife of the noted character, Sam Conn, owner of the equally notorious Green Goose tavern at Newburg in the early days of Knox township.

The farm site is a quiet, drowsy one, nestled in a lonesome, soggy, rough valley covered with elder, willow and locust thickets; but its past history and a terse knowledge of those who lived here tints it with a solitary, sombre background rather gruesome and uncanny even in these late days.

* Thorp, Harvey D., "Taylor County History and Folklore," *West Virginia Folklore*, Fairmont, WV., XV, 3-4 (1965), pp. 36-37.

The narrow, rough road that passed near this house was never travelled much when first built, and a century later was abandoned and made a dead-end lane for those who cared to travel it — and at night few ever did, due entirely to its shadowy past.

* * * * * * *

It was here at this spring at Sally Fisher's Fork that Cooper built his red brick house when he entered this region in early 1800. Other settlers coming to take up their homesteads were usually hardy frontiersmen who had seen service in Indian wars and had endured a life of rough living. They found Cooper's dealings were as close as the hide of a woodchuck or the bark on a stunted hickory sapling. Selfishness was a trait incompatible with neighborliness so they quickly passed him by. No one cared to help him with his harvest nor did they care to call at his house. Cooper never attended a public meeting in fear he would in some way have to share a paltry penny or do some service with no remuneration. Few knew much about him, but many as much as they cared to know. The nearby elder at Hale meeting house expressed his views by saying his actions would be verified by that trite, ancient adage. "He that is greedy of gain, troubleth his own house." Never did the elder make a better prophecy for Cooper's evil ways, like a pestilence, spread, and in many ways the innocent suffered more than he with the calloused soul.

An old Jewish peddler became a frequent visitor in the Knoxville settlement soon after the town was founded in 1813, and regularly continued his visits for the three decades following the second War of Independence. He had been a soldier in that conflict and many of the citizens of Knoxville were his comrades — in war only — and had fought with him in the Battle of Lundy's Lane on that twenty-fifth of July, 1814. Often when in the village these warriors would meet at the post office in James Clear's house and hear the Jewish patriot tell the true version of that fierce and bloody fight. . . . It was here he lost his leg. "Old Pegleg" was the resulting nickname.

Knoxville, for a century of time, was a village of intolerance to creed, politics, and race, and old Pegleg, the peddler, was frequently presented the key to the village by a shower of ancient eggs. The elders of the church had often ordered him from their doors by the shout of "Christ killer." Although considered a racial and religious outcast he was a familiar lonesome figure on the landscape, carrying his large pack of merchandise. Although cattle and dogs would be carefully taken in at night, old Pegleg would have to seek his lodgings at night at the red brick on Croxton Run. Cooper always awaited these trips with greedy satisfaction, charged the limit, and gave in return as scantily as possible.

It was long rumored that the old peddler was very wealthy and carried all his life's earnings in his money belt. But of this he never proferred a word as to whether his supposed opulence was fact or visionary. For years he made his monthly trips and by necessity always stopped at the insidious miser's house. This was continued until one cold, blustery January night in 1830. That old Pegleg had disappeared was the talk of the neighborhood.

That same spring the parsimonious owner of the red brick bought a nearby farm, paid cash, and promptly moved into the new domicile. His shady reputation, scorched as it was, followed him, but the heavy shadow of suspicion and mystery still clung about the old house that only became darker and more baneful by the passage of time.

Cooper soon urged a renter to move to the vacated brick. This renter soon became slightly mentally deranged and this only added fuel to the general connotation that all was not right at the little valley house.

The renter's wife dolefully recited that the entire cause of her husband's trouble was hearing many times each night the footsteps of a man apparently with a pegleg walking up the front stone walk, but invariably disappearing before reaching the front door steps of the house. Many times her harassed husband would open the door to welcome the stranger but he would invariably disappear. The renter would be standing ruefully noting a large luminous spot on the walk which by day was transformed into a vivid red spot.

A new renter moved into the house and soon weird, unexplainable things began to happen. One night the renter and his wife attended the nearby village church and on their return the children were frantic with fear. The youngsters not only claimed they heard, but that they saw, the peddler coming up the walk and that he entered the front door, passed down the hallway, and upstairs to his room. They described the peddler so accurately and minutely that they were afraid this was no figment of their imagination.

Later this new episode was widely heralded over the countryside as signifying that some misfortune had in some way overcome this Jewish peddler, and that undoubtedly it was his indomitable spirit back in search of his hidden body. Whether the crime was accidental or premeditated, when put as an interrogation, was met with an accusing shrug of the shoulders and a far away dark look of bewilderment. All realized that with Cooper, money, no matter how acquired, was his idol of worship. As for the case of the peddler, later actions lent belief that Cooper knew more than he had yet revealed. From this time on he was looked upon as the embodiment of all that was malicious and evil, and in truth he acted his part in this drama on a background of his own creation.

One foggy night a few doubting Thomases stood guard along the walk leading up to the house and remained until they lost their courage completely and made haste to Knoxville. To them half of the melancholy story had never been told. That night this second renter assisted them in the watch until nearly midnight when his eldest son would be returning from Knoxville where he had been sent on an errand. He casually stated to these watchers that it was usual each morning to find the barn and stable doors wide open as if someone had made a complete search of their contents; that noises in the attic of the house were so frequent and loud that his querulous children refused to sleep under the attic roof but slept their restless, disturbed nights on the floor downstairs where they claimed that they also heard continual noises like someone digging with a pick.

Finally old avaricious Cooper took ill with a disease he felt was to be fatal. For the first time in the memory of the oldest living person who knew him he requested that someone bring the parson of the nearby hilltop church. He desired to make a confession. It is well he did for that same day he passed on to join the peddler — although few granted him full rights to that happy sojourn.

The minister shortly afterwards found two elders in his church he could trust, and armed with picks and shovels began to excavate in the cellar of the old brick. Strange to relate they knew exactly where to dig and soon found a few bones, buttons, and buckles which they carried outside and buried under a large flat rock without the benefit, but at the suggestion, of the clergy.

The pastor then gravely remarked that in 1787 an Indian battle had been fought here. But it was an oft-debated question in farm houses and village stores whether Indians in 1787 wore trinkets such as were found. A second question equally debated was why this old reprobate gave of all things, a donation to the church duly, but very quietly, accepted.*

My Grandfather's Story

My grandfather, Neri Swetnam, was born in 1813 in the Big Sandy Valley of eastern mountain Kentucky, a decade after his family had come west across the mountains from Virginia. He was religious, and proud of his reputation for truthfulness. As a young man he made a trip on horseback through the wilderness to visit his ancestral home and family, the trip referred to here. This is his story as told in 1890 to my mother, Flora Stafford Swetnam, who told it to me.

Night overtook me as I was riding along in a very wild area, but I determined to keep moving forward in hopes of finding some stopping place. Late in the night I sighted a light, and found it came from a large house. I called, and a man came to the door. After I had told my plight, he said: "I don't want to turn you away, but the only bed I can offer you is in a room said to be haunted." I told him that didn't

* Schilling, Robert W., *Tales of Yellow Creek,* Gold Seal Publications, Poland, OH, 1942, pp. 128-35, 138-39.

worry me, and he showed me to a clean room, where I was soon asleep.

Before long I either dreamed or awoke to find someone was trying to pull me out of the bed. I fought against it, and it went away. Later I was again awakened, this time by a young woman with a lamp in her hand, who beckoned me to follow her. I did, and she went down the stairs and out into the yard a little way and pointed to a large stone at the foot of a beech tree. Then she disappeared, and I returned to bed and fell asleep.

Next morning I woke early and went outside, where I saw the beech tree of my dream, with the stone at its foot. I turned it over, and underneath I found several pieces of jewelry, including a ring, so small I could only get it on my little finger, and then not all the way.

Just then the man came out and called me to breakfast. While we were eating, he saw the ring and suddenly turned very pale.

"Stranger," he asked, "where did you get that ring?"

I told him about my dream and about looking under the stone and finding the jewelry.

"Stranger," he said, "that was my dead wife's ring. We could never find it after she died."

* * * * * * *

From that time on, members of the family have seen, or heard, or otherwise experienced what appeared to be visitations of the supernatural.

Between the family home and the village of Blaine, KY, a mile away, was an old wooden bridge where it was said a man had been hanged in the pioneer days, and where strange things often happened. Teams of horses or oxen, usually tractable and well behaved, would often shy there at night or even in broad daylight, and could hardly be forced by the whip or goad to cross, although nothing could be seen.

At the time my parents were married, my father's two brothers, Joseph and Hamilton Swetnam, were still single and living at home. The younger, "Uncle Ham," was a big man, over six feet tall, and so strong that the town bully once said: "I'd rather be kicked by a mule than to have Ham Swetnam hit me with his fist."

One evening after supper, Uncle Ham had walked over to the village, and on his return was overtaken by dark. The family heard him come running at top speed, and he jumped a four-foot paling fence into the yard rather than delay to open the gate. Although it was late October and the weather was crisp, he was out of breath and in a lather of sweat when he reached the house. He would never tell the reason for his haste, although it was well known he wasn't afraid of any man on Blaine Creek, armed or unarmed.

Uncle Joe also experienced something at the bridge once, and ran the half mile home.

"Just after I had crossed the bridge," he told my mother, "I saw something in the air beside me. I hit at it, and it was suddenly on the other side. I struck at it with both fists, but couldn't touch a thing, and it was suddenly in a different place. Flora, I'd rather be hurt than scared that bad. I just ran. It kept beside me for a short way and then disappeared."

My father, William Wylie Swetnam — (a number of boys in Kentucky, Ohio and West Virginia were given the name William Wylie in the middle 1800s, but I've never learned for whom) — and a friend were sitting up one night with a very sick old neighbor man, my father told me in my youth.

Deep in the night the friend had gone outside, complaining of the July heat, but for a purpose anyone who grew up in the mountains without plumbing would understand.

"Suddenly," my father told me, "I saw something like a black cloud floating over the bed, and then it passed out the door. I ran out and Martin told me he had just seen a black cloud come out the door and disappear. When we went back inside, the man was dead."

In 1940 I was living near Uniontown, PA, and had gone to Blaine in August to see my father, who was nearly 78 and in poor health. He was still able to get up and walk, but was very much troubled because although his mind was clear, he had almost completely lost his ability to talk. I went to see his doctor in the county town of Louisa, and asked him about the situation.

"I really can't tell you much," he said. "He's getting food and nursing, and that's all that can be done for him. He might live two years, or he may be dead when you get back to the house."

About six weeks later I woke just after 1 a.m. after a very vivid dream that I had been at his house. He came out on the porch to meet me, wearing bib overalls, and with a smile on his face. "George," he said, "I feel well, my mind's clear, and everything's all right." Later I learned that he had weakened suddenly and died at just that hour.

The beat goes on. After we moved to Pittsburgh in 1943, our two children, George, about 7, and Anne, four years old, talked of a "Miss Mattimer," a gentle poltergeist, who apparently moved with us when we moved to Glenshaw in 1950. One day when I was alone in the house and I was toweling myself off after a bath, the bathroom door suddenly swung open, although it was a bright summer day, with not a breath of wind. For no ponderable reason, I almost automatically said: "Miss Mattimer, that isn't nice." And at the word, the door, which had come wide open, swung gently shut again.

Not long afterward our other ghost made his appearance. George, then about 14, asked me one day: "Dad, did a Revolutionary War veteran ever live in this house?"

Obviously the answer was no, since the house was only built in 1885, so I asked the reason for the question.

"Sometimes when I wake up at night I see a man in a long, black coat in the room," he said. "He stands there for a minute, then steps up to the foot of the bed, looks out the window, and disappears."

Further inquiry made the description seem like an 1890's businessman in a Prince Albert coat. And I knew that the house was built for James B. Kirk, an official of the Baltimore and Ohio Railroad who was sent here to keep an eye on Henry W. Oliver, who was building the Pittsburgh and Western with B&O money. And the window looked out directly on that railroad.

Little was said further of the matter until years later, after George had married, and his younger brother John, was sleeping in the big bedroom. I had mentioned the story to a friend at a party, who asked: "Has anyone else seen it?"

"I don't know," I replied. "Nobody else has slept in that room but John."

"Has John seen it?" the friend asked.

John was standing beside us, so I turned and asked: "Have you, John?"

"Yes," replied John, "I've seen it." His mouth closed like a steel trap, and I knew red hot pinchers couldn't draw another word out of him, on the subject.*

Little Beaver Ghosts

A century ago ghosts were everywhere, with some localities more prolific than others; of these the many old Indian camps around Cannelton, Negley, and Frederick were celebrated. Also the smaller graveyards so common everywhere though surrounded with cultivated fields yet with their maze of briars and unkempt grass plots, they gave an atmosphere which required little imagination to fill with phantoms holding high carnival within their precincts. At one of these graveyards, noted for sculptured headstones, there is held an annual conclave of ghosts, often seen marching in and around the graves, four abreast, led by a noted stage driver, Jeff Whippo. Several of these ghosts seemed to be at variance with their fellows, wandering about solitary and alone, haunting vacant buildings and out-of-the-way nooks and corners.

One manacled with chains, wrapped in an Indian blanket, with long gray hair, has by nightly strolls through the house frightened so many tenants that the ancestral McMillan homestead overlooking the Little Beaver, has stood deserted for years. Near the opening of Cannel coal mine three ravines meet with small rivulets and rocky falls, marking a dark but lovely spot. The music of Whip-poor-will falls, coupled with the groans of "Oohche, Eacchi," from beech fiddle trees

19

* George Swetnam

as the wind sways them together makes the cry of dying victims. Here the first McCaskeys settled in 1793. The father, a Whig, was killed in South Carolina and the family driven into exile by the Tories and British dragoons under Tarleton. The family located a settler's claim over the Cannel mine, building a log cabin also clearing a few acres of land. One of the daughters named Barbara, was handsome and had two suitors. One morning Barbara, was found murdered and her head missing. Her ghost is erratic, sometimes the body, or only the head appearing at unlooked for times and places. Only a few years ago a driver of a four-horse team related in all sincerity an encounter with Barbara. Coming down the cross roads from Hell's Hollow Tavern, he observed a dark figure and when right opposite the apparition, it sprang upon the back of the off wheel horse — a gray beast that enabled him to observe the outlines of a headless woman. On reaching the old McCaskey cabin site the woman sprang off and disappeared in a glow of bright light. What convinced the driver that there was no deception, [was this:] a cold night his horses were in a lather of sweat and trembling and ever afterwards his team would shy on passing this cabin. Barbara's sister Mary, afterwards married and is buried just across the Ohio state line. Even after death Mary continues an (sic) "Xantippe of Wife" and troubled her husband by ghostly appearances. To appease her spirit the tormented husband erected the elaborate headstone.

*   *   *   *   *   *   *

At Long's Run we have the ghostly appearance of a heroic pioneer saving his family from a burning cabin and the Indians. At the canal lock below Vondergreen's, little Gretchen has often appeared murmuring her dying prayer "Bury me with my mother," and in the deserted stone mill at Sprucevale, on St. Nicholas eve, the ghost of Esther Hale, the Quaker Lady preacher, appears and rewrites on the stone wall her old text, "Come."

Conrad Weisner, (sic) Pennsylvania's honest interpreter in 1748, made a journey into Ohio and stopped on the Beaver river attending a ghost dance of the Indians. Each dancer wore a white robe or shirt and all claimed to have seen and held communication with the spirits of departed friends.*

The Phantom Encampment

Some years ago, probably around the year 1934, a young couple were walking along one Saturday morning on a road near Ambridge, Pa., known as the Legionville Hollow Road. They were on their way

* Mansfield, Ira F., ed. Robin Hood Club, *Historical Collections of the Little Beaver Valleys, etc.,* (Beaver Falls, PA: 1914), pp. 215-17.

to do their shopping in Ambridge, and it was broad daylight.

Suddenly the two saw a blazing fire, flames shooting up in the air, and around the fire figures, dancing in and out among the flames. Other figures could be seen sitting around the edge of the fire.

The couple were so frightened they started to run. "It must be something we imagined," they said to each other when they had passed the place.

But just then a truck came up behind them and the driver, when he got to the couple, stopped his machine.

"Did you see what I saw?" he asked, his face white. And he proceeded to describe the very scene that had so startled the couple.

All three were sure now that what they had seen must be real. Could it, they wondered, have been a ghostly encampment by the soldiers of General Anthony Wayne, reenacting a scene that had taken place here long ago? Or Indians, dancing in celebration of a victory, won here back all those years? Who can say?*

The Ghost of the Packsaddle Gap

"Whaur is the New Mune? Ech, here you are, my dochter — I feel your warm breath on my brow; but I canna hear your footfa' by my side. But then I couldna hear nae mair the new mune walk across the sky when last I saw the glint of the fair sma' thing in heaven — when last I saw you, dochter, comin' doun the hill — a fair sma' thing on earth — A New Mune of love to your mither sightless frae that hour to the new mune of light aboon. Dinna min' that waefu' day, lassie, when your fayther's poother brunt in my loof wi' a spark frae my luntin' pipe? Weel, weel, God's gude — His wull be done!

"Ech, here you are. I ken that cough, an I canna hear your footfa' on the flure — you move sae light. Aye, aye, I ken that cough too weel, dochter. It is an echo frae your fayther's grave! But God's gude — His wull be done! We'll a' meet again, and sune.

"That cough again — I would to God that I were deaf as weel as blind — Nay, na; God's gude — His wull be done! It was His gudeness, dochter, to spare me the sight of my pale New Mune gangin' backward into night — to leave me een to weep for your fayther and see na his dochter's wraith. But it's a road we a' tak' — God's gude — His wull be done. I am thankfu', dochter, I canna see the light of your een and the red, red rose in your cheek, when the bird i' the birk at the dure is singin', and not Tam Skelton on the mountain brae.

"Ah, Tam, Tam! He's a wild an' wilfu' callan, dochter; but his heart is in the right place. He's been a comfort sin' your fayther's gone — your fayther, lassie, loved him an he waur your brither, and blessed

* Gruszczynski, Joseph, "The Phantom Encampment," *Keystone Folklore Quarterly* VI:4, Pittsburgh, PA (1961), p. 2.

him wi' the words that dribbled frae his lips — till he spak' nae mair. But dinna sob, lassie, you canna luve the lad and it be not God's wull. Dinna sob, lassie; he'll coom again. He canna be far awa'. The deer that hung at the dure the morn — dinna ken, lassie, whose bullet sped to its heart? Your fayther, lassie, taught the lad to shoot — your fayther, lassie, gie the lad his long gun wi' his blessing. And Tam may whyles be dark and glowrin', yet his heart is in the right place — he luves you, dochter — he luves you weel. Nay, na; dinna sob sae in dool; you canna luve the lad in return an' it be not God's wull — and God's gude, dochter — His wull be done.

"That cough again — I dinna wunner, dochter, your cough is waur the day. Tam Skelton brought nae the roots wi' the deer that hae eased your cough before; but I dinna think that his thoughts were not about you, lassie; for he luves you. I am bleert and blin', an' my hearin' is thick, but I feel in my heart, that is weel and strang, Tam Skelton luves my dochter as Donald McDowell loved me. Sae dinna sob, lassie; he will coom again, when, if it's God's wull, you'll learn to luve him as he luves you.

"That cough again! Coom, dochter, and lead me to the birk, nigh the dure o' the biggin, and I will point with my tremblin' finger to the place on the mountain brae, whaur Tam has gathered the roots for you before — whaur your fayther, lassie, taught the lad the worth o' the worts that grow there — the crottles o' the rock, and the roots i' the ground.

"There — dinna see, ayont the river, on the mountain brae, the tall cedar tree that stands alane, wi' its tap amaist aboon the mountain height? There, lassie, gae and gather the roots that ease your cough as they did your fayther's before you. Gae, lassie, gae; and I will sit i' the sun till you return; and though I canna see you cross the foord and climb the hill, I wull know and feel that the New Mune winna forget to glint at her blin' auld mither atween her steps. A kiss — there — now gae, and my blessing be wi' you, my bonnie New Mune of luve on earth. God's gude — His wull be done!"

The old woman said: The widow of Donald McDowell, a hunter frae the Highlands of Scotland, who settled in the heart of the Packsaddle Gap many years before the building of the Pennsylvania Railroad through that picturesque mountain gorge — many years even before the construction of the Pennsylvania Canal through that monstrous rent in the walls of the Chestnut Ridge, which for ages the Conemaugh river has been cutting and keeping open for the great highways of civilization to come — who settled there in a log cabin, his wife and his daughter, Maria, his only family; his long rifle, his only means of support, besides a massive sleuth hound which he had brought with him from Scotland — Bruce, so gentle in the cabin, so terrible in the chase — gane to his lang hame wi' his master, noo.

Maria crossed the Conemaugh at the ford, on the great stepping-stones which had been adjusted in the brawling river by her father and Tam Skelton; and och! the eerie look which she gave herself in the mirror of crystal water in the nook on the opposite side of the stream from her mother! — a slender bow of flesh and blood — a glint of pearly lustrous white — a New Mune on earth as faint and fair as the first glimpse of the new moon in heaven! — and yea, as pure and holy in thought and deed as that which the new moon in the cloudless azure symbolizes in the heart of man!

Now, now, thou bonny New Mune of love to thy blind auld mither, leave the mirror of the river, and hoolie, hoolie, with heated breath, ascent the mountain side to the cedar, and gather the snake root and pipsissewa, and — God's gude — His wull be done!

The New Mune, weary, and panting for breath, reached the shade of the cedar, and stood at rest with her hand against the bole of that single tree of its kind to be found in the Packsaddle Gap, when, the report of a rifle reverberated through the gorge — and drowned in its echo the faint shriek of Maria McDowell pierced through the bosom by a bullet from the long gun of her father, in the hands of Tam Skelton, whom her father had taught to shoot — whom her father had taught to go to the very place where she stood to gather the wild roots for her cough — whom the last words of her father, with his blessing, led to that place to provide for the wants o' the New Mune and her minnie while Donald was awa'!

Tam Skelton, the moment the New Mune stopped to rest, came to the brink of the ledge of rocks above her; and, observing through the boughs of the cedar what he supposed to be a wild turkey on the ground — and to signal to the heart of the New Mune and her minnie in the cabin that the last words of her father were not forgotten, and that wild Tam Skelton was not far away, he directed the long gun of the old hunter at the object which he saw, and fired at the bosom of the daughter of Donald McDowell — the bosom of her who was the New Mune in the only heaven which he knew, the cabin of her blind old mother, in the depth of the Packsaddle Gap.

"Nay, na, Tam; dinna tak' your ain life in your hand — think o' my puir auld mither i' the biggin alane! Your hand must hand the spune to her lips; your hand must lead her frae the gloom o' the chimney-neuk into the warm light o' the sun; your hand must tuck the flannel at night about her shiverin' limbs; your hand — some day, not far awa' — must wrap the white shroud round her banes and lay them i' the cauld earth by my fayther's! — your hand, Tam, has bluid enough — bluid enough! Dinna dip it in my mither's wi' your ain! It was God's wull; it is His wull; I dinna score you, Tam, wi' ony thought o' sin; God's gude, an' och, Tam, I ken you luve me dearly.

"Nay, na, Tam; dinna touch me — let me lee whaur I hae fa'n, under the cedar whaur my fayther's luve and care brought us thegither to this deadly meetin' — it was God's wull! But brak nae word o' this to my mither, ava, ava. Say I am gane — nae mair — and gie to God the lave o'it!

"Nay, na, Tam; dinna touch me. It is eneugh to feel your scaudin' tears fa' on my face and neck. I leuk into your greetin' een, and see your heart and luve for me — but dinna kiss me, Tam! When I am dead — tak ae — nae mair! — then lave me whaur I lee. For, Tam, dear Tam, I canna luve you in life as I would; as I wull luve you in heaven, an the New Mune luik doun an' see Tam Skelton kiss my lips but ance an' nae mair, an' then lave me whaur I lee, and gang to my puir mither, and say, the New Mune is in heaven — God's wull be done!

Tam Skelton took on his lips the last breath of the dying girl; and then — he knew not how — he descended the mountain steeps and crossed the river — and told the blind old mother that the New Mune was in heaven — and tucked the blankets about her shivering lumbs — and staggered out at the door — and into the wood — and lay insensible on the ground through a night of lightning-blaze, of thunder-crash and flooding-rain!

When he awoke in the morning, and gathered about him his bewildered wits, he heard the roar of the Conemaugh as he had heard it never before! He looked, and lo! a mighty torrent was rushing through the mountain gorge, overflowing the banks of the river, and sweeping everything before its extending reach into an engulfing flood of destruction! The cabin was in danger, and its helpless inmate. He ran — he waded into an eddy of the torrent to his neck; when the cabin melted into a mass of drifting logs and clapboards and puncheon flooring! — and there, amid the bounding timbers — what was that that made Tam Skelton's eyes start in their sockets? — an arm, outstretched toward the New Mune in heaven, of the blind old woman, muttering beneath the wave, "God's gude — His wull be done!"

The wretched man shrank backward through the turbid water of the eddy, keeping his eyes fixed on the timbers of the cabin until they disappeared in the bend of the river; when, looking up, he beheld another horror, and a greater — one that remains to this day in awful grimness and weirdness, as it was revealed for the first time to Tam in the flood! The lightning bolt had shivered the great cedar to the ground; the torrent on the mountain side had swept the body of Maria into the flood below; while the ledge of rocks, concealing before behind the boughs of the cedar, stood out in bold relief the features of Donald McDowell! — the husband of the blind old woman who, but a moment ago, had disappeared in the flood — the father of the fair and holy one who the day before had fallen before the muzzle of his own gun, in the hands of her lover, whom he himself had taught to shoot — the foster father of Tam Skelton, to whom, with the last words which he spoke, the dying hunter committed for protection the helpless wife of his bosom and the tender child of his heart, Maria, the New Mune on earth — now, in heaven! — the grim features of the rugged hunter of the Alleghanies to be seen to this day in the jutting rocks of the Packsaddle Gap, where the sprays of cedar grow, and there only, in that mountain gorge of the Conemaugh — the features of Fate fixed in the mountain rock!

The waters fell; the Conemaugh shrank into its narrow bed; the stepping-stones appeared; but Tam Skelton never crossed the stream and ascended the mountain side to the place where he had taken ae kiss — nae mair — and fled; where the father of Maria McDowell forever afterward looked at him as he had done on his death-bed when he gave him his gun with his blessing — to kill his own daughter by the hand of her lover, and to drown his aged wife before the eyes of the torrent-stayed victim of fate!

What became of Tam Skelton — the wild and wilfu' callan of the blind and auld mither — will never be known perhaps. It is believed, however, that he has never left the gap, and that, an old, old man, he walks to and fro along the banks of the Conemaugh to this day — stopping for a few moments, every time that he passes the face in the rock, to look at it, his left hand grasping the end of a long gun, like a staff, and his right hand, while holding the rim of a bearskin cap between his thumb and forefinger, pressing against his upturned brow, at the same time easing his racked brain, and shading his blood-shot eyes from a glance, perchance, of the New Mune in heaven! There are old men still living who, while hunting in their youth on the mountain crest, have looked down and beheld the wretched man thus stand and stare against the side of the mountain as if his eyes were riveted on something that suffused him with agony, and then disappear in the woods. And so, there are middle-aged men, still living, who remember that, while the canal was still in operation through the gap, the mules on several occasions started back in affright and leaped into the water, giving way to the spectre of an old man that emerged from the bushes and strode along the tow-path until he came to a point opposite the face in the rock, where he stood and stared, as above described, and then passed on and out of sight. And so there are men in their prime to-day, engineers on the Pennsylvania Railroad, who, while swinging around the curve at the mouth of the Pack-saddle Hollow — the wildest and the weirdest point on the railroad in the Gap — have seen, with the most appalling horror, an old man step on the track before the locomotive and stand, leaning on a long gun or staff, and stare at the mountain side through the increasing gloom of approaching night, and see not the glare of the headlight until — horrible! horrible! the old man is ground beneath the wheels! Thrice already the train has been stopped at this point; and thrice the engineer has descended from the cabin, and, with a sickening heart, walked back along the ties in expectation of finding the mangled remains of an old man lying on the track — on one or the other side of the roadbed — or on the declivitous side of the mountain along which the railroad has been cut — or a hundred feet below on the bank of the river where he might have been hurled, and where humanity bids the search be extended; but the light of the lantern has not revealed to the engineer, nor the light of day to the laborer, the mangled body of wild Tam Skelton — the weird old man that haunts the Packsaddle Gap and sees forever the Features of Fate in the ragged outline of the jutting rocks on the mountain side where the cedar sprays grow — while the New Mune gleams in heaven!*

The Re-Appearing Ghost

It seems that many years ago an old man by the name of Albert Wiles, who lived near Thornton (WV), was walking home from work late one night. (Albert worked in the coal mines and didn't quit work until after dark.) On his way home this particular night, he noticed a small boy, with a green-hooded coat, walking along the road. Mr. Wiles naturally could walk faster than the boy, so he caught up with him. He asked the little boy what he was doing out all alone this time of night, and the boy told him he had been to his grandmother's and was on his way home, but he had gotten lost. Mr. Wiles noticed that there was blood on the boy's coat sleeve, and he found out that the boy had cut his finger on a briar sticking out in the path.

Mr. Wiles found out that his name was Billy Skiles, and he told the child that he would take him home. When he heard this the boy disappeared and could be found no where. Naturally Mr. Wiles was disturbed by this, so he went to the Skiles' home to see if the boy had gotten home. When he knocked at the door an old woman came to the door. She informed Mr. Wiles that her Billy had disappeared some thirty-five years before, and that he had a green-hooded coat, which was found in the woods right after his disappearance.

She took Mr. Wiles to the closet, and there they found the green-hooded jacket, with fresh blood on the sleeves!**

The Johnson House

The old house which stood on Mulligan Avenue had been vacant for several years — ever since old man Johnson had died that horrible death in the attic. It had been a strange and horrifying occurrence. It seems that a mysterious slayer had stabbed him to death and cut his heart out. A thorough investigation had been made, but no one was ever charged with the crime.

Now, ten years later, Mr. and Mrs. Burns were going to buy this very same house. Since they were new in town, they had not heard this terrifying story. The Burns' moved in that week and nothing

* Cowan, Frank, *An American Story-Book* (Greensburg, PA: 1881), pp. 61-68.

** Thorp, Harvey D. M., "Taylor County History and Folklore," *West Virginia Folklore,* XV:3-4 (1965), p. 43. (Attributed to his great-grandfather.)

seemed to be unusual until one night a couple of weeks later Mrs. Burns heard some strange noises in the attic. Mr. Burns had left earlier that evening for a trip to New York City, where he was a salesman.

Mrs. Burns was naturally terrified at this noise, so she ran to her bedroom, and locked the door. She pushed a chair under the doorknob and then climbed into bed, hiding herself under the covers.

She remained very quiet for what seemed like hours, because she was afraid of who or what might be in the attic. Finally she pulled back the covers, only to find her bedroom door standing wide open. On the floor were spots of fresh blood which led down the steps. Since it was daylight now, Mrs. Burns followed the blood spots down the stairs and on down into the basement.

When she finally got into the basement, she saw rows of catacombs of the Johnson family. The blood led past these to a corner of the basement. The blood stopped right in front of a clothes rack which had belonged to Mr. Johnson. Located beside the clothes was a catacomb bearing the name of J. C. Johnson. Mrs. Burns touched the clothing on the rack and found that it was still warm from perspiration, and the blood on the clothing had not dried yet.

It is believed that Johnson roamed the house for many years in search of his heart.

A few years ago the old house burned to the ground, and it is believed, to this day, that Johnson struck a match to look for his heart, and caught the roof on fire.*

All houses wherein men have lived and died
   Are haunted houses.

— *Henry Wadsworth Longfellow*

Some Pittsburgh Area Ghosts

This is part of a report on letters to Radio Station KDKA following a Halloween broadcast on area ghost stories.

Often they were about the length of this one from a Bridgeville woman:

"During her last illness my aunt lived with my mother. She and her nurse had rooms on the first floor of the house, with a bath between. My mother slept on the second floor.

"One night the nurse heard a man's voice singing a hymn. It seemed to be coming from my aunt's room. The voice was clear and strong. The nurse heard it clearly though both doors were closed.

* *Ibid.*, pp. 41-42.

"The next morning, when the nurse told her about the experience, my aunt said: 'Yes, my father was here last night. He had some young boys with him, and they were singing his favorite hymn.'

"We all felt that Grandfather had come back to my aunt to comfort her. The visit did seem to reassure her. She passed away two weeks later."

* * * * * * *

A good many of the stories seemed to be connected with the approach or danger of death: A Bridgeville man about to go out for the evening with friends saw his dead aunt, who warned him not to go. He stayed home, but two of his friends died in the crash of their car. An Apollo woman, well educated and a student of psychology, was warned in dreams before the death of her mother and brother. A woman on Howe Street (and she gave her name and address) told how her husband — now dead 10 years — returned and talked to both her and her daughter.

From Alliance, Ohio, a woman told of being visited in her home two years ago by a man who had been strangled with a leather strap. After she had moved to her present home, shortly afterward (and she gives her name and address) he came there and sat in a chair. "I am not a medium," she added, "and I do not know how to call spirits. I am not a spiritualist — I am a Presbyterian."

A Washington County woman wrote: "After my father died, he continued the practice he had in life, which was always tucking the covers in around my mother when she went to bed. Mother said this went on for four months. She was never scared, for some reason, although she never saw him, but felt his hands doing their nightly chore.

"She talked to our priest about this, and he advised her to ask Father what he wanted, or why he was not resting. Mother did so, and then he materialized and spoke. He said: 'Susan, the National Bank,' three times, then vanished.

"Mother waited two or three days, then went to see the banker. She found that Father had left us $2200, which she never knew he had. Mother was left with seven of us to keep, so you see it sure was a God-send. This happened in 1920, and Mother says Father has never come to her since."

Another letter:

"A woman from Sharpsburg told me of the ghostly visitor she saw in 1932 in a house on Main Street, where a former occupant had hanged himself. She located the building quite accurately, and it is still in use."

Many of the accounts referred to happenings at houses which are still standing, and whose numbers were freely given. One, at least, is reported to be empty because no one dares to live there. Other people seem to be able to live with ghosts very well, for years, seeing and hearing inexplicable things without being frightened.

* * * * * * *

A couple in Port Washington, Ohio, told of an experience which occurred when they went a few years ago to visit the wife's uncle, whom she had not seen since childhood. Last year they visited him again, and just after leaving they picked up a hitch-hiker, who turned out to be a cousin. He rode with them for about ten miles, gave his name, and talked cheerfully with them about family history, mentioning many facts she knew, and some others she learned later were true. They promised to visit him this year.

She thought little of it until last July when they visited the uncle again, and mentioned picking up the cousin, and what he had told them.

"He told you the facts all right,"said her uncle, "But it must have been the first time you were here that you saw him. He's been dead several years now."

"I usually do a good job of driving from the side seat," she added, "telling my husband not to drive fast, and to be more careful. But until we got home, I didn't need to say a word."*

The Lost Hand

The area of Prickett's Fort was continuously being occupied by settlers who were searching for land on which they could farm and land that they could call their own.

The family of Thomas Evans was one of the first to homestead the land along the Monongahela River.

With less than thirty miles to go before reaching the fort, the Indians attacked Tom Evans and his family. In order to save his wife and four children, Tom sent them ahead while he stayed behind to fight the Mingo Indians.

After waiting three days for Tom to reach the fort, his wife Jemima, set out with a search party to find her husband. Much to her sadness, she found Tom hanging up-side-down from a tree — dead. The scout of the search party couldn't figure out why the Mingo Indians, who always scalped their victims, hadn't taken the hair of Tom but had taken his left hand.

Even though she had lost Tom, Mrs. Evans settled down at the fort to await spring. By spring, the Evans' family had decided to stay in their new home area. Within three weeks, the men built them a home, and they were becoming accustomed to their new life.

* Swetnam, George, "Our Pittsburgh Ghosts," *The Pittsburgh Press,* Pittsburgh, PA, October 25, 1959.

After being in their new home for only two nights, the family was awakened by a scream from a man; a man who sounded like Tom. But it couldn't be Tom — Tom was dead. The following nights were filled with this same strange piercing scream. The beginning of the next week brought the full moon of May, but no scream from a man in pain. The night was clear and calm. The moon was so bright that Jemima couldn't sleep. As she walked out on her porch, she saw something shining in the moon light near Tom's grave. What could it be? She remembered placing flowers that evening on his grave, but there was nothing that would shine! She walked slowly almost as if she were afraid of what she might find. She didn't need the light from her lantern, but she took the gun from inside the cabin and headed for the grave.

Upon reaching the grave, she found that her flowers were still there but holding them was the skeleton of a hand. On the hand, a wedding band shone brightly. She slipped the ring from the finger to find the initials, T. E. E. — Thomas Edward Evans.*

Meeting at Dead Man's Tree

Harry Jones and his family had a cabin not far from the fort. Harry was a good Christian man, and tried to do his share of the work that was expected of the men of the fort.

He and his family had come to this newly settled land for a chance to have their own farm. When they came, they had traveled with a man from the same town where they had lived. The man, Dave Little, had been engaged to be married to a friend of the Jones', and it seemed very strange when they had met him outside of town as they were leaving to journey westward.

Since Little knew them fairly well, he asked if he could travel with them. Being such a good man, Harry even shared their food with him, and the men became good friends as the trip progressed. When the trip was half over, Dave became suddenly ill and died. After a short service at his grave side, the Jones family continued on their way to the fort.

Harry had been in his new home only three months when he began to have a dream — the same dream every night. He dreamed that his friend, Dave Little, wanted to meet him at a tree near the fort at midnight in order that he could tell him something very important.

Harry told his friends of this dream, but they just laughed and said that he must be in need of rest. But the dream continued to haunt him even in the daytime.

* Stanley, Penny, "Early History and Legends of Prickett's Fort," *West Virginia Folklore*, Fairmont, WV, XVI:3-4 (1966), pp. 2-3.

One night when he awoke from having this same dream, he decided that he must go to that tree before the dream drove him out of his mind. So, he put on his clothes and walked to the tree. The night was rainy, and the lightning lighted the way for him. When he was within thirty feet of the tree, the lightning flashed, and he saw a piece of paper under the tree. On the paper the words were written: "I cannot rest until you return her money. You must do this for me." Where had this note come from?

The next day, Harry left for the grave of Dave Little. The answer to his question would surely be found there. When he dug up the grave, he found in the lining of Dave's coat three hundred dollars in gold.

The whole story seemed to fit together then. Dave had stolen the money from the girl whom he was going to marry and had left, never to return. Now in order to find peace, the money had to be given back. Even though Dave was a crook, Harry had to do this last thing for his friend. He traveled to his old community and found the girl of whom Dave had spoken. After telling her the story, he gave her the money and then started back to the fort.

The evening that he arrived home, he went to the tree where he had found the note. When everything was silent, a man appeared saying, "You are indeed a good man. I thank you, my friend." Then he was gone.*

The Fiddling Ghost

Of all the Indiana County ghost tales, however, the most persistent is still that of the Fiddling Ghost of the Mahoning Valley.

Mahoning Creek is nearly twenty miles above the line that ran from Cherry Tree to Kittanning, and marked the land which the British purchased for settlement in 1768, from the Indians. That line has always loomed large in Pennsylvania history, and especially in Indiana County, where "up above the Purchase" is as common a phrase as is "the Mason and Dixon Line" in the south.

The area was settled much later than the rest of Indiana County, and has always been a little different.

On a country road in West Mahoning Township, near Smicksburg and not far from where the Baltimore and Ohio Railroad crosses Mahoning Creek, stands a small house with an unusually high and steeply peaked gable roof.

In this house, legend relates, lived two old men, not brothers or otherwise related, but apparently friends. Both had come into the area to work on the railroad (then known as the Buffalo, Rochester, and Pittsburgh) which was at that time being built.

* *Ibid.,* pp. 14f.

One of the men was a fiddler, who became a popular figure at country dances, barn-raisings, and corn huskings. Perhaps he played at home, too; and this may have gotten on the nerves of his friend. In any event, one day they failed to show up at work, and a search revealed the fiddler stabbed to death, his bow broken, and his fiddle smashed in bits. The other man had fled.

It wasn't long after that time that residents of the district began hearing strange sounds from the house, according to Howard Lockhart of Smicksburg, who has kept track of the matter.

Then rumors began to get about. The men of Indiana County are taciturn men, not quick to talk where they may not be understood or believed. But one after another at last began to admit that he had passed the house and looking up had seen the ghost of the dead man sitting astride the roof, playing his fiddle.*

Yank Brown's Deathbed

Mrs. Frances Strong Helman of Indiana, who collected the lore of Indiana County (PA) ghosts, believed the first case on record there was the ghost of "Yank" Brown — or rather the ghastly appearance of his reputed victims.

Perhaps it is significant of Indiana's spiritual plenty that the Yank Brown apparitions used to haunt the old Northern Pike Road in the county's southwest corner, exactly "andy godlin" from the location of the more famous Fiddling Ghost.

Few people today, if any, remember Yank's real name. He had come from New England many years ago, and took his nickname from that area.

Yank was the traditional rotten apple out of a good barrel, which may have been one of the reasons why his family — all very reputable people — went on westward soon after his death.

Shortly after coming from New England, Yank started a tavern near Clyde, on the old (Northern) Pike between Blairsville and Armagh.

The tavern appeared to offer good entertainment for man or beast, for that early day. But before long there began to be rumors.

People were seen in the evening coming down the road to the inn, the rumors said, who were never seen next morning on their way again. And Yank and some other questionable characters of the district were said to be driving away and selling some mighty fine horses they had neither bred nor bought.

Yank was given to towering rages at times, when his deadly violence tolerated no living person near him. People in the area still

* Swetnam, George, "The Fiddling Ghost of the Mahoning Valley," *The Pittsburgh Press,* Pittsburgh, PA, October 30, 1955.

point out an overhanging rock near Black Lick Creek, where they say his wife and children had to hide from his wrath. There's a cave, too, where tradition says Yank and his gang used to hide the horses until they could be driven quietly out of the country by night; but no one ever knew where he buried his alleged victims, from whom the horses were said to have been taken.

Perhaps the victims — if indeed there were any travelers murdered — didn't sleep well in their hidden graves. For people who lived in old Wheatfield Township began to hear strange things.

Those who walked along the Northern Pike at night, legend says, used to hear the sound of ghostly horses and drivers. But when the sounds reached and passed them, not a thing could be seen — even if the watcher had the courage to stay and look.

Then came the horrible night when Yank was dying. And all night long, runs the story, the hoofbeats and wheels of unseen horses and wagons, the creaking of unseen harness, and the hoarse shouts of unseen drivers created a turmoil on the highway before the tavern.

Once it appeared that Yank might break down and unburden his soul of the truth. But some of his gang were beside him. "Die game, Yank," they kept urging him, and Yank's lips were grimly set to the last.

For years the sound of the ghostly horses and wagons could be heard on dark nights, until the road was changed, and the roaring of motor cars and trucks drowned out the spirits.*

The Spook of Indian Hill

A short distance westward from where Town Fork, a branch of Yellow Creek, joins with the latter stream there stands a high, rough, once thickly-timbered hill that from the earliest recollection of the pioneer Yellow Creek valley settler has been known as Indian Hill. There, encompassed by flat fertile meadows, it stands like some lonesome discredited object meditating on its past colorful history or perchance the unaccountable uneasiness of those who have dwelt within the circumference of its subtle influence. Between it and the two creeks once flourished a village of redmen. Their wigwams were there in the dim past when all nature was at peace, and the red deer and these children of the forest lived together, co-partners in the ownership of these densely forested hills and valleys. Now, due to the ravages at the hand of the white man, the lush, luxuriant growth of wilderness that clothes the landscape from the rising to the setting of the sun has been shorn and shoved back. Today only a thin scalplock of stunted brush and trees partly hide the summit of Indian Hill.

That this rugged old hill has brought much fear and trembling to the nearby countryside can be told candidly and without timidity

33

* *Ibid.*

of successful contradiction.

In its earlier day, so tradition says, the dome of this hill embraced a small area that was used as a Wyandot burial ground and seemingly it is from this enchanted spot that emanates the mystic incidents that outweigh the nightmares of the most fantastic dreamer.

Maps printed in the middle of the nineteenth century had the same site marked "Indian graves." The earliest owner of this section of land was George Wilson. When he settled in 1799 this hill was then known as Indian Hill and surrounded by a haze of Indian tradition and tales.

From this focal point have issued tantalizing screams, but diligent search has revealed nothing; distressing moans, and no cause found for their being given; let alone uncanny lights and a multitude of other fearful manifestations that have caused intrepid hearts to quicken and courageous souls to ponder deeply. Whether this be caused by ghosts, sprites, specters, goblins, or some other dark, sinister spirit, has never been satisfactorily determined. But the book of evidence is well filled with episodes that none but a select few dare to question the veracity or totally disbelieve. These truths are halting in only a lone particular, that being no one has had the courage to come forth and assert he has been an eye witness to the cause of these uncanny actions. Nevertheless, the causative influence back of these unusual actions has always born the sombre title of "The Spook of Indian Hill."

On the very topmost crest of this eminence, like a huge quill in an Indian headdress, stands an ancient, druid-like oak that has weathered the storms' lashings for at least a half millennium. For centuries it has stood there like an ancient sentinel — yet proud, erect, and alert, although ages ago it had its heart shattered and its mightily outspreading limbs rent from its sturdy trunk by the powerful flashes of lightning that seemingly must strike it another ruthless blow with each passing angry storm. Today it still stands upright, but hollow and limbless from its successive warfare with the elements. It is now a grotesque form as uncanny as the episodes that have been enacted within its shadow.

Why so much mystic, unwritten lore has been associated with Indian Hill, its screams, noises and lights, just because it was a modest, redman's "God's Acre" has never been explained or faintly understood. The sounds are such as cannot be imitated but are always so weird that one and all have agreed that it must be some solitary lingering spirit in distress or one who had met some untimely end in the hazy past, long before the advent of the white intruder into this tranquil valley.

In 1800 the first settler in this valley, Phillip Saltsman, repeated an interesting story told him by a soldier of the Revolutionary War who often travelled the Yellow Creek route to Fort Laurens on the Tuscarawas. It was on May 18, 1780, that this soldier was carrying a message from his commanding officer at Fort McIntosh at the mouth of the Big Beaver. As he was passing Indian Hill he was certain he heard noises resembling the rumbling sound of a passing thunder shower that came from a small part of this hill top. He stood at its base for quite a while to try to ascertain the cause for this unusual sound. As the day was warm and clear it could not have been a thunderstorm. He climbed to the top to see. The sound of heavy thunder still continued but no visible cause could be noted. He wondered what this portent indicated. The next day he believed the sign was made clear and fully explained, for on that day the sun failed to show and the same night the moon had the appearance of a great red ball. It was known as the "Great Dark Day," the cause of grave concern to all then living.

In the spring of 1803 more strange noises, not unlike that of very small children, were heard on the summit of Indian Hill at all hours during the daytime for a period of a month or more. Several inquisitive hunters went up to seek the cause. Outside of finding many grouse they also found the nests of several bald eagles occupied by young eaglets. Some suggested that a wolf might have a den of cubs or that a wild hog might have hid her litter of noisy sucklings in some rocky cavern on the hill top. That same spring it rained every day in the months of May and June, but very few noticed that the two pair of eagles were now accompanied by their four noisy, screaming fledglings in their frequent flights up and down the otherwise quiet valley in their vigorous quest for food.

In 1806, Benjamin Maple, on his road home from the county seat, detected a strange noise, not unlike small foxes barking, on this hilltop. Upon searching he could find no cause for the sounds, although the barking never ceased while he was present. When he arrived home he told the folk about this strange incident and recited a legend told to him years before about Indian Hill.

It seemed, in early days, a Wyandot maiden lived at the foot of this hill and was in love with a Mingo chieftain. As this chieftain was not of her tribe and clan her red father strenuously objected to her marriage to him. In her grief she threw herself from the eastern cliff of Indian Hill into the icy, raging water of the creek below and instantly disappeared from sight. Once each year her dusky parents return, so the legend tells, and stand watching wistfully while plaintively calling for her to return to her people again, thinking that she is only lost in the black, unending wilderness and unable to find her way home.

Those who listened intently to this heretofore untold and unknown story ardently concluded it foretold the advent of new trouble. The anticipated trouble truly enough was brought to light for this hardy old backwoodsman was caught, lost and perished that winter in a severe blizzard.

On the eighteenth of June, 1812, James Andrews, a Virginian, came across the Ohio on a hunting trip in the Yellow Creek valley for wild turkey. This valley was a hunter's paradise and well known as such. Abundantly successful in his trip he was on his return back to the river when he was caught in a torrential rainstorm near Indian Hill. He immediately sought refuge under a large, projecting rock along the hillside to await the storm's conclusion. After the fury of the storm had spent itself he noted the most brilliant rainbow he had ever witnessed spanning the sky from the crest of the hill to his rocky shelter. He enjoyed the brilliant, promising phenomenon and noted exactly where the two ends touched the earth. At that very hour, he later found, Madison's war was declared. He was made a major, performed heroic services for his country and, besides his army pay, was given this same entire section of land over which he saw this bow arched. Here he moved his family and built a cabin, and it was here he lived for half a century an honored, industrious citizen.

In the year 1833, on November thirteenth, strange lights were seen on Indian Hill. The whole top was luminous with a dull, pale glow among the shrubby undergrowth. Some of the more erudite thought it to be some form of northern lights, others that it was sheet lightning. But deep in the hearts of the older people this strange light foretold some catastrophe to follow. That night was a never to be forgotten one, for on it occurred the most brilliant and greatest display of ''falling stars'' in modern times — in fact, apparently all the stars of heaven were in motion and many felt that this was the time of the end of the world so long foretold.

In 1840 this enigma of Indian Hill took on a complete, new, unheard-of procedure so unusual that it was the constant topic of speculation in all the cabins in the Yellow Creek valley; so unaccountable that the most gallant and valorous quaked with abject fear at the recital of each strange, unpredictable act.

One dark, foggy night, in February of that year, old Doctor Andrews was making a professional call in the region of Indian Hill. He was riding along the muddy creek road on his favorite sorrel horse thinking about the little patient he had just left further down the creek. Suddenly he was hit a resounding clap over the head, knocking his old beaver hat into the muddy, icy water of Yellow Creek. He was sure that this apparition was carrying a small chain as he plainly heard the rattle of the metallic links. As the genial doctor was a man of probity, sound judgement and exemplary character, his word was taken at full value. His experience of being struck by a chain by some object travelling in the darkness of night was widely spread throughout the valley.

The Yellow Creek ''wiseacres'' said it was a premonition of something soon to happen. The aged physician from that time on received few calls from the Yellow Creek valley and hills after dusk, and he always noted that no matter how tardy he must be to make the call the messengers would always stay and accompany him back to the patient. None ever offered to see the doctor safely home.

From all the nearby farmhouses came the same awesome narration of hearing the spook with the rattling chain. The story was no sedative to tired mothers or scared children afraid to leave their cabins after the sun sank from the western sky.*

The Missing Knife

The Viola community is located about midway between Montana and Meadowdale (WV). The northern section of this community adjoins the famous fort site and Prickett's cemetery. Only a stone's throw from Viola is an old log cabin that Captain Jacob Prickett and his son built in 1781, still standing in very good condition on the portion of road that leads toward the Montana community. The following legend was passed down through the years from the early settlers of the community of Viola. This story was told to me by Mr. Jack Cottrill who lived in the vicinity of the fort site and Viola for many years.

The Old Wilson farm stood vacant for over twenty-three years. No one dared spend a night there, let alone live there. No one, that is, until John Harvey came to the vicinity of Prickett's Creek. John had been warned of the ghost who had been seen on several occasions, but he did not believe in ghosts.

The first three nights that he spent in his new home, he heard a knock on his door. As he opened the door to welcome his very first visitor, he found nothing — nothing but the wind howling in the trees, sounding as if it were repeating, "Give me the knife. Give me the knife!"

But John was determined to live down this tale of a man who was killed by his wife with a butcher knife. The tale is about Ed Wilson's ghost haunting not only his wife, but also the people who lived in the Wilson place after Mrs. Wilson was found clutching her butcher knife near the gate — dead!

On the fourth night, the moon was full, and John was, for some reason, very jumpy and nervous. At the stroke of midnight, a knock awoke him. He reached for his gun which he always kept close to his bed, and went to the door only to find again that no one was there.

When he started to turn to go into the house, he felt someone watching him. He looked out beyond the gate to see a man staring wildly at him. John yelled, "What do you want?" The man walked toward the fence. Stopping short of the gate, he reached down and

* Schilling, Robert W. *Tales of Yellow Creek*, Gold Seal Publications, Poland, OH, 1942, pp. 141-149.

picked up a knife. Then he smiled, as if he had at last found his peace.

While John stood watching, the man slowly faded into the ground.*

Help

The following story was told to me by my aunt, who heard it from her friend's grandmother. It was supposed to have happened many years ago in West Virginia.

Doctor Anderson was awakened by a persistent knocking at his front door. Accustomed to having his slumber interrupted in such a manner, he dressed quickly and hurried downstairs.

The red glow from the hearth cast flickering shadows through the room. Glancing at the large wall clock, he noticed it was just past midnight. Outside the moon shone brightly on a blanket of white snow.

He opened the door and was surprised to see a young girl twelve or thirteen standing before him. He had never seen her before. She was dressed in a blue coat, carried a white muff, and her cheeks were ruddy from the brisk cold.

"Please come to my mother," begged the girl. "She is very ill, and unless you come at once she will die."

"Who is your mother?" asked the doctor.

"She is Mrs. Ballard," replied the girl, "but please hurry."

Then the girl explained that she had only recently moved to the old Hostler place about three miles away. She said she feared her mother had pneumonia and, since her father was dead, there was no one else to come for help.

When the doctor assured her that he would come at once and do all he could, the girl darted away, running up the road in the direction of the old Hostler place.

Doctor Anderson bundled up in his sheepskin coat, pulled down the ear flaps in his cap, picked up his bag, and went to the barn for his horse. He lost no time in throwing on the bridle and saddle, picking up a blanket because it was "blue cold," and heading for the Hostler place, for in those days pneumonia was a dreaded illness.

As he hurried his horse up the cold snow-covered road, he mused at the bravery of the young lass who had braved the severe cold to seek his help. She had flitted away before he could recover enough to ask her in to warm herself before starting home, yet she hadn't appeared to be cold.

His thoughts soon turned to his own discomfort, because his feet and hands felt numb and near-freezing before he saw the glow of a lamp in the old Hostler house.

* Stanley, Penny, "Early History and Legends of Prickett's Fort," *West Virginia Folklore,* Fairmont, WV., XVI:3-4 (1966), pp. 5-6.

Quickly tying his horse to the gate post, he threw the blanket over it, and hurried up the snow-covered walk to the porch. There was no answer to his knock, so he opened the door and walked in. The sight was a common one to him. There in a bed lay a very sick woman. The fire was almost out, but the oil lamp still burned. He felt the woman's pulse, noted she was awake, and saw that she carried a very high fever.

He placed more wood on the fire because the room was cold, then set to work with the skill and confidence that comes from having handled many emergencies. He knew if he could break the fever he could possibly save this woman's life.

After giving her medicine, he heated water and applied poultices to her chest. She soon rallied enough to whisper audibly and asked, "How did you know to come?"

The doctor replied that her daughter had come for him and that she was a brave girl to go out on such a bitter cold night.

"But I have no daughter," whispered the woman. "My daughter has been dead for three years."

"I wonder who it was," mused the doctor; "and how did she know you were ill? She was dressed in a blue coat and white muff."

"My daughter had a blue coat and white muff," whispered the woman. "They're hanging in the closet over there."

Doctor Anderson, being a practical man capable of scientific thinking, strode over to the closet, opened the door, and took out a blue coat and white muff. His face went ashen and his hands trembled when he felt the coat and muff, still warm and damp from perspiration.*

The Invisible Collier

After Lewis' forge went down some fifty years ago, several coal pits were made close to its ruins and Jacob Isenhour, one of the colliers claimed that one day, when he was busy digging on one side of his coal pit, he heard somone on the other side shoveling, and when he went around, no one was to be seen. He then went to shoveling on that side and he heard someone digging on the side he had left. He dropped his shovel and hurried round, and no one was to be seen. This thing was repeated all day. When Isenhour was on one side the noise would be on the other side. If he was digging the noise would be on the other side. If he was shoveling the noise would resemble someone digging, but no dirt was dug or shoveled, and the pit was in a cleared off space of several yards; so no one could come from the surrounding woods and escape back again. Some years afterward,

---

* Bradley, Terry, "Help," *West Virginia Folklore,* Fairmont, WV, XIII:1 (1962), pp. 2-4.

not far from Isenhour's coal hearth, a man by the name of Smith and a companion were at work on a coal pit, and digging for dirt by the side of a large rock a few feet from their coal pit, they dug up the bones of a man. Some supposed that this was Isenhour's invisible helper; while some suggested it was the remains of the wagoner, who drove his unearthly team where mortal man dared not to venture.*

The Man from Hogback

This particular incident happened in Rowlesburg, West Virginia, about seven years ago. My present landlord, Mr. Norman Mankins, lived in Rowlesburg then and was head of a company that was assembling a television cable line. "Moose" Mars was employed by the same cable company, and along with a few others, he was with Norman when this event occurred. (Moose got his name from his large size.)

Mr. Mankins, Moose, and about four others were watching television in the company's work shack on top of a hill called "Hogback." It was about 11:00 p.m. when they heard something outside tearing down the bushes. Most of them thought it was a deer. Norman was curious, so he went outside for a look, and as soon as he stepped out of the door he called to the others to come outside.

When they came, they were shocked to see a man about six feet, eight inches in height, and as stock as a bear. It wasn't his build that shocked them, but it was his face. Norman said that it was the strangest-looking thing he had ever seen in his life. The man or monster had a greenish tint to its skin, and appeared to have animal-like features about its face.

Well, the monster was standing about twelve feet from the men, and was making "strange noises." They stood like that for about a minute, when Norman asked the man or monster what he wanted. The monster just growled and started advancing hostilely toward the men. "Moose" Mars grabbed an axe from the company's shack and said, "If you want trouble, we can give it to you, but if you're friendly give us a sign."

At that point the monster drew back his arm and hit a tree about three inches in diameter, and it burst into splinters. That was enough for Norman and the others. They ran into the shack as fast as they could and locked the door. They watched the monster leave — after about five minutes, in which the creature knocked down about five trees with one hit of his hand for each. As soon as he was gone, Norman and the others made the fastest trip off Hogback that they had ever made.

* S. T. W. (S. T. Wiley), "Legends of Fayette County," *Genius of Liberty,* Uniontown, PA, March 31, 1881.

About an hour after the men got home, the whole town of Rowlesburg knew what had happened and was in an uproar. The town council held a meeting and decided to have a posse formed for the next night — to try to catch the creature.

The next night about 150 men were on Hogback with flashlights and high-powered rifles, but this posse failed to turn up anything.

A lot of people didn't believe the men had seen any such creature, but I know them all and if they swear they saw a monster-man of that description, they did!*

Slag Pile Annie

In the early 1950s a young student from the University of Pittsburgh had a summer job at one of the large steel mills in the Pittsburgh area. His particular job was to run a motor "buggy" through a tunnel under the steel furnaces after they had been drawn, and gather up the hot slag from the furnaces in the hopper cars in his train. After he had gathered a load he would drive his train out on the dump and deposit the slag.

It was a dark and dismal place down there, in spite of the occasional electric lights.

One day as he was driving his slag train below the furnaces he noticed a woman standing beside the track a short distance ahead of him. She was dressed in coarse clothes and wore a red bandanna tied over her hair.

The young man stopped his buggy and said, "Lady, you'd better get up out of here. You're likely to get killed down in this place."

The woman turned toward him and said, "I can't get killed. I'm already dead."

The young man got down off his buggy and went upstairs immediately and sought out the foreman. He told him about a woman being down in the slag tunnel and repeated what she had said to him.

The foreman asked him to describe the woman, and when he heard the young man's description he said, "Oh, that must have been Slag Pile Annie. During the war when laboring men were hard to find, we hired some women to do certain jobs, and running that buggy was one of them. This Slag Pile Annie ran that train you now operate. She was killed in an accident down there about five years ago.**

* Baumgardner, Richard, "The Man from Hogback," *West Virginia Folklore* XIII:1 (1962), Fairmont, WV., pp. 10-11; as told to him by Norman Mankins.

** Turley, George, "Slag Pile Annie," *West Virginia Folklore* XV:1-2, (Fairmont, WV: Fall and Winter 1964), p. 16f.

Joe Magarac

The legend of Joe Magarac, the mysterious, gigantic steelman, has been much abused in recent years. It has been altered and plagiarized in print, sometimes by writers of note on folk matters; it has been misused for propaganda purposes, and for advertising, much as was done with Paul Bunyan. It has even been disputed whether there ever was a real folk-hero Joe Magarac — some arguing that the whole story was an invention of Owen Francis who wrote the first published account for Scribner's Magazine *of April 1931. One principal ground was that no folk hero would ever be named Magarac, which means "jackass," disregarding numerous instances of such naming, as for instance, the Norse god, Thor ("fool").*

No one had been able to contact Francis on this matter. All we know of him are the notes he gave the magazines when these and several other stories of similar type were published half a century ago. They say he was born in 1898, wounded in World War I, worked in Pittsburgh mills, tried scenario writing in Los Angeles, began one or two novels, gave up writing, and returned to mill work. Actually, there may never have been an Owen Francis, except as a pen name. [It can happen. More than one bibliography has listed work by Acker Petit, which happens to be one of several pen names of George Swetnam.] Whoever the author was, he had evidently worked in a Pittsburgh steel mill, and knew the folk.

Those who question the fact of such a folk hero have failed to recognize that, while Francis was the first to publish a story about Magarac, other trustworthy sources report knowing the tale many years earlier. One is the Hungarian-American poet, George Szecskay, who says the legend grew out of one Andrew Katonah, a Hungarian who came to America at the time of the civil wars in his native land, and was nicknamed "Joe Magyaron" (Joe, the Hungarian). Another and much fuller account, unquestionably authentic, was published in the **Western Pennsylvania Historical Magazine** *in 1944 by George Carver, a University of Pittsburgh professor. His chief but not sole source when he worked in the mill in student days about 1909 was one Gregor Stepanovich, a Yugoslav, who had heard the tales in his youth many years earlier.*

The story, evidently genuine, appears to have arisen from the wishful thinking of immigrant workers who — with all the cards stacked against them — needed some hope to lean upon. And the designation Magarac would appear to come from the unionizing efforts which ended disastrously in the Homestead strike of 1892. Union organizers did not want the workers to rely on a mythical hero, but upon the union, and so represented Joe as big and strong, but too dumb to join a union, or even get married — a man whose only wish was to eat, work, and sleep.

43

Gregor in his grotesque speech revealed the rudiments, at least, of a character worthy to stand alongside the heroes of no matter what romance; for it symbolized ideal accomplishment, summing up as it seemed to do the hopes and the will to succeed — far short though most of them fall — of a body of men whom all of us have realized lived among us but very few have come to know.

Joe Magarac — the name has no significance as far as I could learn — was born of the mists that hover over the lakes and mountains of the "old country," and of the coal and iron of America. He is thus endowed with the strength of the earth but also with the elusiveness of air. He is as large as occasions demand but fleeting as mist in the sun. He moves with the speed of light; rather, he seems to occupy whatever space he chooses without moving from spot to spot. He is at times the immovable body, and at times the irresistible force. He appears in the midst of workmen taxed beyond their powers and with an effortless push or lift overcomes their difficulty; only, when they look around to see who has helped them Joe Magarac is nowhere to be found.

In the course of time Gregor told me a great deal about him. One of the stories had to do with an incident in the open hearth. Gregor had heard it from one of his countrymen when first coming to work in the mill but the man had long since wandered off to Rankin or Homestead — Gregor could not remember which.

About four o'clock one afternoon Number 6 furnace was, as usual, ready to tap. The men were all in their places, ready to add sand or dolomite in case the slag should harden too rapidly. The plug was removed and the first splashes of molten steel struck the bottom of the ladle. But something was wrong with the flow. The heater was back on the floor peering through his blue spectacles at the white hot charge to see what was damming the stream. He finally began to poke about with his long rods and things improved somewhat. The flow was not normal, however.

When the ladle was about three-quarters full, it all happened. A menacing hiss and the rear wall of the furnace split just above the vent, cascading a torrent of steel, bright as liquid sunlight, into the huge pot. Since none of it escaped to threaten the workmen or be lost on the floor, nothing seemed amiss — the wall itself could easily be repaired. But the craneman had no sooner lifted the ladle to place it over the ingot molds — the story deals with open hearth practice now long outmoded — than a crack started up near the brim. The sudden pressure had been too great and the ladle, designed to receive a gradual flow, had developed a defect. The crack widened with the motion of the lift. Another second and the whole heat would have poured down upon the men. With a single, concentrated shriek of terror they wheeled in flight. Yet they stopped upon the instant, stopped and stood as if transfixed, motionless like figures painted upon the shadowy wall of the open hearth shed.

For one among them — whom later no one could remember ever having seen before — appeared to assume the proportions of a giant. Torso, shoulders, head, arms were magnified enormously and thrust upward upon shaft-like legs to tower above the fifty-ton ladle as if it had been a saucepan. The giant grasped the lips of the crack, one great hand upon each, and ground them together so that at once the ladle was made whole again. Not a spark remained visible, not a splash of fluid steel overflowed. Order was restored. Aware of their escape from the scalding death, the men, who but instants before had shrieked in terror, now shrieked with joy. But they fell as suddenly silent. The ladle was being moved along in normal fashion. There was no giant anywhere. They looked at one another with eyes for the moment insane. Were they awake? Or did they dream? All that remained to remind them of what had passed was a thin mist of steam that arose from a puddle where some of the hot metal, in the beginning had fallen.

Whenever during the days that followed some trifling emergency arose I would wish for Joe Magarac, but Gregor would only smile; nothing short of imminent disaster involving life as well as property would bring him, it seemed. And then one morning, just as we were starting to work, the runner laid an order for five hundred kegs of eight-penny common nails upon my little movable desk. Such an order was the simplest we handled. It meant that Gregor only had to touch each keg with the stencil and brush and see that the kegs were placed in ten rows of twenty each in both ends of the car, leaving five rows to be placed across the middle to hold the others in place; my part being merely to see that among the five kegs each trucker brought nothing but eight-penny common was included. Gregor was delighted at beginning a day in such fashion. He laughed and said, "No Joe Magarac this job. But one time he helped with eight-common. On barge." And then because there was ample time between trips from the car to the stock pile, he could tell me the story.

The company maintained warehouses in various cities to facilitate local shipments. One of these was located in Memphis. The stock was loaded in a huge covered barge and shipped down the Monongahela, the Ohio, and on to its destination upon the Mississippi. The barge held some forty carloads, or twenty thousand kegs. Upon this occasion the whole order had consisted of eight-penny common, the nail, of course, in largest demand. The kegs were loaded in cars in the usual fashion and pulled down to the loading wharf a mile or so away, there to be reloaded in the barge. The work was not unpleasant, for the most part in the open air instead of in the vast, gloomy warehouse, and the men always enjoyed it. There was seldom a mishap beyond an occasional smashed finger if the kegs hurtled down the slide too

45

fast — from the trestle to the hold of the barge — or beyond an infrequent ducking, when one of the men in an awkward movement fell overboard, much to the glee of his friends.

On the last day of this particular job, according to Gregor, because of spring floods the river had swollen so much that the barge was almost level with the trestle instead of lying, as it should have lain, much lower by reason of its lading. Furthermore, pressure of the water and its more violent motion had caused the mooring ropes to fray. In the midst of a sudden downpour of rain, the men on the trestle stampeded across the shute into the barge for protection.

Their sudden, added weight rocked the barge, heavy though it was. It swayed away from the wharf and the mooring ropes parted — to permit the unwieldy and uncontrollable craft to be sucked swiftly into the flood current. There was no steering gear aboard, nothing in any way to be used either to stop the barge or to control its direction. It gathered speed with every passing moment and everybody aboard knew that there was every chance of being wrecked in a crash against the close-set pylons of a bridge not a hundred yards downstream. But, in mad career one minute, in the next the barge stopped and remained stationary. Then it seemed to be propelled backwards. Gradually it was pushed back to the point from which it had started. A dozen men jumped out upon the wharf to make it fast with the badly frayed ropes, and one of them, glancing toward the middle of the river swore he saw a swimmer who turned his head toward the shore and waved a gigantic hand. But all anyone else could see was a faint mist rapidly dissolving in the rain.

Eventually Gregor told me about the time when Joe Magarac saved a workman's life by catching a filled ingot mold when the crane that was carrying it jammed and broke the chain; about his using his fingers for twelve-gauge dies when all the dies in the wire mill would draw nothing but run-outs; and the long story about the tram of pig-iron that broke loose from a donkey engine and started down grade toward the main office. In fact he had many stories, some of them not without a grotesque, obscene humor. But the exploit I have always liked best had to do with Joe Magarac's rescue of a small boy who carried water for the men engaged in building Number 12 blast furnace.

Gregor had forgotten the boy's name, and he was certain that the family had moved away soon after the event — I could never manage to tie him down in matters either of narrators or witnesses. The small boy was something of a pet among the men on the job. They permitted him to do about as he pleased, go where he wanted to, and ask anyone questions — so long as his water bucket was at hand and freshly filled. One afternoon toward quitting time, he decided he would mount a long ladder rising from the ground all the way to the gadgetry at the top of the furnace. The work was almost completed. Number 12 was about ready to be blown in, but some of the scaffolding was yet in place and a number of ladders remained. This one alone reached the top, however, some eighty feet from the ground.

The boy was almost half way up before anybody noticed what he was doing. Then one of the riveters saw him and shouted for him to come down. The boy merely looked around and laughed. The riveter continued to shout and in a minute or two a crowd had gathered and the whole group began to shout. But for a time the boy paid no attention, going on up rung by rung until he was sixty-five or seventy feet from the ground. The shouting increased as he proceeded, and once more he turned to look down at the excited crowd. But as he did so he became ill. Dizzy with a sense of height and growing faint, he stopped where he was and merely hung on. As the men watched they saw him slump against the ladder. If he fainted completely he would fall the long way to the ground. The crowd plunged into a turmoil of activity. Some ran for another ladder. One rushed to telephone the fire department for a net. Everybody shouted, some offering advice, others exclaiming in fear. Finally, the riveter, a man used to climbing about in high places, placed a foot upon the ladder, thinking perhaps that he could reach the boy before he should fall.

But before he could mount two rungs, a dark, powerfully built workman appeared whom nobody seemed to know — the bystanders, Gregor explained, were all mechanics engaged in construction work and so were alien to the steel itself; hence they could not have been expected to recognize Joe Magarac — nevertheless it was he. Nobody else could have done what he did. For, brushing the riveter aside, Joe Magarac lifted the ladder slowly so that the ends of the stringers rested upon his thighs. Then, grasping the third and fourth rungs, he turned the ladder about in order to clear the towering furnace and brought it very gently to the ground, the almost unconscious small boy near the top describing a wide arc in which he was brought to safety. Many hands lifted him as he reached the ground, and he was taken into the company hospital, where he was soon brought around in good order. In the excitement of the rescue nobody thought of the rescuer. When at last somebody did look around for him, he was not to be found. The whistle blew at about that time anyway, and everybody went home. Several of the men noticed, however, that the steam rising from the whistle was very dense that day and seemed to remain longer in the air than usual.

Tall stories, to be sure. It may be that Gregor made them up and that the vague repetitions of them that I now and then heard from other men were only echoes of his yarns. I doubt that they were Gregor's own. I rather think that they sprang from the common source of legends — pride in the thought of what men might do if their powers were extended to perfection — and were the accumulated thoughts of many men. Steel is a mighty force in the lives of those who know it. Why should it not lend itself to romance?*

Haunted Roads:

A. The Spectral Deer

On the eastern edge of Wharton Township in the early days about 1798, Job Clark (who kept the Twelve Springs Tavern farther on) built a cabin, and his son Leonard kept a place for travel. In a few years it burnt down, and people claim that a woman in white, after nightfall, could be seen to appear and disappear close to the burnt cabin. About a hundred yards east of the burnt cabin, where a township road crosses the track of the Braddock Road, various parties claimed, years ago, to see something appear in the road like a deer — a shadowy appearance — which they called the *spectral deer;* they said, if riding or driving, something would seem to come up against them, and jar them, and then the spectral deer would appear a few steps away and vanish before their eyes. Bullets fired at it had no effect.

A short distance east of the spectral deer's vicinity, in Henry Clay Township, the old settlers said, in the dusk of the evening, on the side of the road in the brush, some one could be heard pouring coins down upon the ground. A great hole dug there still remains visible, but the money hider still came after the hole was dug and rattled down his coins.

When the National Road was completed, his satanic majesty, from some real or fancied insult offered him by the pike authorities, would not transfer his patronage to, or honor the new road with his presence. Being choice of his company, he may have objected to travel the new road on account of so many Congressmen passing over it on their way to Washington.

Fifty years is the natural lifetime of most ghosts; with houses torn down and roads changed they generally disappear, but his satanic majesty does not seem inclined to conform himself to this natural order, as Mr. Curtis McQuillen informed me that parties claim at this time to see the woman in white, the spectral deer, hear the miser pouring down his coin, and the devil's wagon rattling along close to the burnt cabin, and then changing its course of travel and moving off at a lively dash down towards Shepherd's glade. The wagon running over the cliff of rocks on Pine Run, the wagon rattling down the ford on Sandy, and the team of the Prince of Darkness careering over the old Braddock road, are nothing but noises closely resembling the running of a wagon, and when fully understood, they will be found to be

* Carver, George "Legend of Steel," *Western Pennsylvania Historical Magazine* 27:3-4 (1944), pp. 132-36.

produced by some natural and not by an unnatural cause. They are interesting subjects for scientific investigation.*

B. The Braddock's Run Spirit

The memories of Braddock's run, where a retreating army camped and buried whatever of their wounded that died that night, naturally made an impression on the minds of the superstitious, who would pass that way at night; and but naturally under the circumstances, their fancy furnished what their imagination suggested — and soon after the National road was built it was whispered that where the National road crossed Braddock's run a misty shape of a man would accompany persons across the bridge on the run. After many repetitions, report improved the ghost by increasing its dimensions and deepening its outlines — making it a very large soldier man to be plainly seen walking by your side till you crossed the bridge and then vanishing; but speculation never came in this case (as they do in so many,) to complete fancy's creation, by assigning a reason for his nightly appearances, of revealing his crimes that chained him to earth after death.**

C. The Pedler Rocks

After the Braddock road crosses the National Road some two and a half miles on the north, between the old Downard stand and the old Cushman tavern stand, on the left of the road, are high rocks, or rather a ledge of rocks; and here on these rocks about the beginning of the nineteenth century, a pedler was killed — his wagon run off and his horse turned loose. This story was enough to excite the fears of the timid and cause predictions by the superstitious, and in a short time some wagoners reported seeing a man all bloody standing on the rocks and moaning; others claimed to see him, and some to hear him and only seeing nothing; but when the National road was built and the Braddock road vacated, the spirit seems to have been released from his nightly exhibitions or else being lonesome, left. For years nothing has been seen or heard of this spirit. In the natural course of events in a few years, the last of these lingering spirits that cling to the old Braddock road in the darkness of winter's storms and the lightness of summer's bright moon beams, will bid farewell to their loved haunts — as man's reason rises above his superstition — these spirits will be heard of no more, only as myths of the past.***

* Wiley, S.T., ''Legends of Fayette County,'' *Genius of Liberty*, Uniontown, PA, April 28, 1881.

** *Ibid.*

*** *Ibid.*

D. The Ghost of the Seven Loops

This is a story which was told to me by my father. It had been told to him when he was a small boy living in Summers County, West Virginia.

There was an old man who hauled salt from the salt wells in Charleston to stores in Hinton, which are about sixty miles apart. The old man hauled the salt on a road wagon, that was drawn by a large team of horses. On his route he traveled a section of road which was called the loops. The loops consisted of seven short hills, with steep slopes on all sides of each hill.

On each of the old man's trips, he had to cross all seven of the loops. One night when he had crossed the seventh loop with his load of salt, he was beaten to death by someone unknown. The murderer did not take the salt, horses, or wagon. The horses and wagon were found about a mile along the road, when the horses became frightened and ran away.

It has been told that at certain times of the year, one can hear the horses and wagon racing through the loops. Some people have said that when they were walking or riding through the loops, they have heard the noise of racing horses behind them, but when they turned around to look, there was nothing to be seen. The noise would keep coming toward them, and then pass by them as it continued down the road.*

The Ghost in the Clock

This occurred in the little mountain town of Mill Run, where I spent my childhood, and when I was yet a young girl; although I was not present, I heard of the event soon after it occurred.

My aunt and uncle had lived near us for many years, and when he died their daughter, my cousin, was away. One of their prized possessions was an old grandfather's clock, kept for its early associations, although its wooden works were broken, and it had not run for a long time. On his death bed my uncle kept looking at the clock, and shortly before the end he told them: "I'm going to come back some day, and communicate with you through that old clock."

No one really understood what he meant, until the first time my cousin returned to the old home after his death. As she and her mother were sitting in the room, exchanging memories of my uncle, the old clock suddenly started to tick — not regularly as when the clock had kept time, but erratically, as if carrying on a conversation. After this had gone on for several minutes, the clock stopped, and remained

* Stickler, Richard, "The Ghost of the Seven Loops," *West Virginia Folklore,* Fairmont, WV, XV:1 and 2, p.11f.

silent, as it had been for years prior to this incident. It never ran again.*

The Ghost Dog

My grandmother and my parents lived in the little mountain town of Mill Run, Fayette County, Pennsylvania.

For years they and many of their neighbors used to see a dog following them near the old Mill Creek Bridge in the village. But it was no ordinary pet or stray mutt. This dog, a large, long-haired one, would follow for only a short distance and then suddenly disappear before their very eyes. This was a source of village talk, but without explanation.

After a long time they learned that in earlier days a shepherd coming through the village with his dog had been murdered. After that they always said it was the shepherd's ghost dog looking for his master.

Perhaps at last the dog found him, for it has not been seen for a good many years now.**

The Ghost at New Geneva

New Geneva is not without its own history of the supernatural — a compelling story about the ghost of a wandering peddler who was murdered around the turn of the 19th century.

In fact, the tale and its sightings were so rampant that in August 1911 "The Pittsburgh Dispatch" sent reporter H. G. Lawrence to Fayette County to cover the story.[1]

He wrote, "In the early days of Fayette County, it is claimed a murder took place on a part of the Friendship Hill farm near New Geneva, now owned by J. V. Thompson, and tradition hands down the weird story of the Peddler's Ghost which for years haunted that neighborhood and appeared frequently to mystify and frighten the people."

According to Lawrence, the murder took place on the farm of a wealthy bachelor named Thomas Clare, who lived in a fine stone house overlooking the Monongahela River and was fond of horse-racing and entertainment.

No one knows who murdered the peddler or can recall the peddler's name. The story goes that the murderer turned the peddler's horse loose and sunk his wagon in the river.

---

* Swetnam, George, (written from an oral history told to a friend by Charmaine Stickel, a former Mill Run resident.)

** *Ibid*

[1] I have not been able to find this story in the *Dispatch* file.

Lawrence wrote that years later a human skull was found on a river sandbank by employees of the Gallatin glass works. The find gave rise to rumours that the head was severed from the body by the murderer and buried separately or that the rest of the skeleton had decayed.

Soon, the Clare house acquired a very haunted reputation until it was finally torn down by new owner Charles E. Speer of Pittsburgh, who wished to rid the land of the haunted reputation.

The house hauntings had included bright red stains that appeared on a stairway windowsill and a fireplace mantle. The windowsill stain was in the shape of a bloody hand; the mantle stain was in the shape of a bloody knife. And no matter how often the wood was scoured, the stains never went away.

Lawrence also reported the house was filled with unnatural sounds of spooks flitting about, doors creaking on hinges and windows opening when everything else was quiet. Outside — usually at night — horses could be heard coming from the sand bank, trotting at full speed. But no one ever saw anything. Once, two young men reported hearing the hoofbeats approaching but only saw dust rise from the ground when the sound of the beats reached beside them.

It was also said a big, black dog haunted the spot where the skull was found. The dog never barked, but followed behind people until they watched it suddenly disappear.*

JOHN
REDDICK
PENNSYLVANIA
ENSIGN 5 CO 2 BN
WESTMORELAND
CO MILITIA
REVOLUTIONARY WAR
WAR OF 1812
1756   1830

* "A Human Skull, Red Stains, A Mysterious Dog," *Voice of the Mon,* California, PA, March-May 1985, p. 13.

Devil Tales

Having seen the devil and been rode by witches.

— Mark Twain

Belief in devils, demons, imps, and evil spirits is far older than civilization, and belief in such fiends today is far from being limited to the ignorant. Most churches officially believe at least in Satan, some in a much wider spectrum of evil spirits. And in more than one denomination the catechumen seeking full membership is required to renounce "the Devil and all his works."

While not so wide spread in the Upper Ohio Valley as ghost stories, devil tales of considerable variety are and long have been occasionally told among the folk. Some ascribe various names to the activities involved, including besides Satan such demons as Moloch, Belial, Mammon, Beelzebub, Asmodeus, but more frequently to unnamed demons, sometimes in animal form, or invisible. The devil may appear in person, may speak a message, or may only be inferred from his activities.

Judge Reddick and the Devil

*This legend, long in folk transmission in the area in somewhat varying forms, involves a well-known historical character who fled to the frontier, became one of the first judges around 1800, and suddenly walked off in the middle of a case in 1830. This version, written by Harry Moore, a small-town editor, and published in his **Vagaries Virginian**, East Liverpool, Ohio, 1910, and **Early and Later Lore of the Ohio Valley** twelve years later (both paperbound pamphlets, now very rare) has been rewritten to some extent from his extremely flowery style.*

You say there went a line of fire round yonder
  Knob, or Crown, or crest?
On such a ghastly night as this the ghostly
  horseman's on his quest.
Hark to the din! See, see them now —
Circling the haunted mountain brow.
Cling to my hand the closer, child,
And I'll relate the legend wild.

— Harry Moore

Far in the hills, where Beaver County meets the border of the West Virginia Panhandle, lies the legend-haunted, almost forgotten tomb of Judge John Hoge Reddick.

Hero of two wars, first associate judge of his county 150 years ago, Judge Reddick was in real life perhaps the most eccentric man who ever sat on the bench in Pennsylvania. And though time has grown so long that his real name is often confused, legends about him are so strange and weird that the hearer may doubt whether to laugh or shudder.

Judge Reddick is said to have been the son of a Virginian who was killed on one of the raids on Fort Henry, now Wheeling. His mother died soon afterwards. Some suppose he was born in 1756 and fought in the Revolution, but his Christian name would indicate he was born close to the time of that conflict, in the region around Washington, Pa. He is also said to have been a colonel in the War of 1812, but no confirmation can be found. He appears to have become involved in a swindle over supplying troops in the Indian wars of the 1780s and fled to the wilderness to escape prison.

John H. Reddick was associate judge of Beaver County from 1804 to 1830, and had a reputation for being rough on fake claims of land companies, and good at getting friends to patch up disputes outside of court. Once he charged the grand jury so eloquently that the jurors asked to have the charge printed for the use of future members, and this was done though no copy can now be found.

Also, at his own request he was buried in the strange tomb at the State Line.[1]

So much for history. How much of the rest of the story may be true or false, no man knows. But the story is one which has been told on stormy nights and by dying fires for more than a century in the hills of Hanover Township, where he lived and died.

Judge Reddick, so the story goes, was a bachelor, with but one admitted passion outside his work — horse racing.

[1] (South of Hookstown, go south for three miles on SR 0168 at intersection of U.S. 30 at Laughlin's Corners; turn west for two miles on Harden's Run Road (SR 3032) to Ross Road; thence three-fourths mile to private lane and property. Ask permission of owners of brick chalet.)

Daily during court terms he rode back and forth between his home and Beaver, though the distance was twenty miles and more, and at his farm he built a beautiful race track, to which came the best horseflesh from what was then "the West." Seldom was there a meet in equine circles in which he failed to figure as backer, starter, stakeholder, or rider. And he usually won.

Judge Reddick's favorite mount, the story relates, was an imported gray stallion of unusual size, bone and power; vicious toward all but his master, who loved to display his tremendous speed.

That became his bane.

Winner once at a great free-for-all, and distancing all other entries, Judge Reddick shouted in a pitch of exultation:

"Not in all Hell, nor yet in this terrestrial zone, neither in the celestial kingdom — no, nor in the winged Devil himself is there evolution to overtake me, once mounted upon my matchless, incomparable, gray stallion steed."

The boast was heard by the demon Asmodeus, arch-fiend of nether air and magic, who at once became obsessed with a desire to punish the judge in keeping with his offense. So irate was the demon that thereafter he kept an imp in limbo to remind him daily of his determination to avenge the insult.

That wasn't going to be so easy. For in earlier days the judge had studied magic to the n'th degree. At St. Clair's defeat in 1791 he had been protected by an invisible blanket, when all around him the Indians were overtaking and slaying other men. And at Tippecanoe he had been accompanied by a dog that showed knowledge far beyond human ken.

His first discovery of the Devil's plan was revealed to him in the buzzing of an insect as he sat upon the bench, judging a case. Whereat he rose without a word, saddled his horse and rode home, and the courts knew him no more.

He sought far and wide until he found an opal amulet which would always reveal what his great enemy's plans might be. He then prepared to build a tomb which would be an impregnable defense.

He first thought of putting it on Round Knob, a few miles west, and one of the highest spots in Ohio. But studies revealed that this was already a demonic Gibraltar, in the hands of his opponent. (And, indeed, to this day there are other stories of the Knob's being an accursed place.)

Instead he chose another spot, nearly as high, on the knob opposite his own home. And there, directly on the State Line as then surveyed, he built a cut stone tomb, ten feet square and of the heaviest style, with a stone floor.

Firmly believing in transmigration of souls, the judge revealed certain signs and symbols to his former slave concubine, by which he might be known in any form in which he might return.

Having died, he was buried as directed in his will. This was that he should lie in a chestnut coffin, open at both ends, directly across the State Line, his head in (then) Virginia, and his feet in Pennsylvania. He was buried on a cold December day in 1842, although some say it was soon after he left the bench in 1830.

But tellers agree that when Asmodeus came for his prey, he was for a time thwarted. For Judge Reddick stood upon his legal rights and refused to be taken out of his state without extradition.

When the demon brought extradition papers from the Governor of Pennsylvania, the judge scuttled out of his coffin, into Virginia. And when a requisition was presented in the Old Dominion, he slipped back into the Quaker State.

Asmodeus used all his arts against Judge Reddick, loosing Siberian cold, tornadic tempests, Saharan heat, torrential flood to dislodge his prey, but all to no avail.

Then he was minded, if he could not catch so superb an antagonist, to enlist him. He knew well that even in life the judge had been an avowed agnostic, so he tempted him with the most seductive elements of all time: Power, glory, wealth, food, drink, and unlimited revelry. But the jurist, in death as in life, was proof alike against all bribes and threats, fear or favor.

At last the demon by some devilish quirk managed to secure a joint writ of extradition from both states, to whose sheer legality Judge Reddick had to submit — true jurist that he was. But still before Asmodeus could serve it he had to catch his man, and the chase lasted twenty-four years — so long that a groove was worn in the tomb's stone floor by their flying feet. During those fearful years neither beast nor bird came near the tomb. But always to be seen close by was a hissing serpent.

Having caught his man, Asmodeus gained revenge by changing him — into a gray stallion, the very counterpart of the one whose race had caused him to make his proud boast. And though the race track was long deserted, hunters passing that way at night would hear the thunder of hooves, and wails of agony as the steed was ridden along, mid the demonic laughter of his satanic master.

Then the servant, his former slave, was wakened one night by a half human neighing, and at the door found a great, gray and amorous stallion, which gave her to understand by prearranged signs that he was the judge, returning o'ertaken; the doom he feared, upon him. He had been rewarded for a good race by being permitted to visit her.

Other visits were allowed by the grim rider to reward bursts of speed, but the girl was physically and mentally unable to stand the strain, and lamenting her master's fate fell into melancholy and died.

Thus endeth the legend. And if you have any doubts, you may climb to the high knob in the old Carson oil field, back of Kendall's Crossroad, and see for yourself.

There, marked by the initials of generations of the curious, still stands the stone tomb, covered with ground myrtle and set about with thorn bushes. And its location must cause the Devil himself to curse each time he sees it, for had he only known the truth it would have saved him years of effort at extraditing the judge.

For when the boundary line was resurveyed about 1882, it was discovered that the tomb is — by a good ten feet — wholly within Pennsylvania!*

Duryea's Death

There was a graveyard on the top of the hill on our farm, above the house. All of my relatives are buried there, and many of the neighbors. Briers and weeds had grown up about the tombstones. I used to pull them away and read the epitaphs on the stones. I recall one: "Remember Friend, as You Pass Bye, as You are Now, so Once Was I. As I am Now, so You Must Be. Prepare to Die and Follow me." I do not remember who was buried there, but it does not matter. The epitaphs were usually not selected by the deceased, but by surviving relatives, and they did not always express the character or views of the one who slept beneath them. I early became acquainted with ghost stories and have been thrilled by their recital by some calling neighbor, around the old fire place at night. Night is the only time that a ghost story should be told. A ghost story told in the day time never has an appreciative audience. There have been many good people who have lived and died in the belief that they had seen ghosts. My father did not believe in them, but my mother would have believed in them if it had not been for the influence of my father. I will never forget old John Ainsley's ghost story of Richard Duryea. Duryea lived alone in a large white house on the Dean road. He had been a sailor and was believed to have been a pirate. In those days a man's wickedness was estimated by his profanity, and by that test, Duryea was a very wicked man. He never went to meeting and never mixed with the neighbors. He had boxes and relics of the sea and his profanity was dreadful. He used to be heard singing "Three Dead Men and a Bottle of Rum," and another sea song about walking the plank. The few preachers who went to see him, barely escaped without assault, and from all of this, the opinion prevailed, that he was in league with the devil, and he was avoided and shunned by all. But he was taken ill and the old woman neighbor who occasionally went to his house to rid it up, reported his illness, and old John Ainsley and Andrew Kriner went to see about it. They found him very ill, and insisted on a doctor, but he would not have one. The night he died Ainsley and Kriner

* Swetnam, George, "Two Southern Beaver Legends," *Keystone Folklore Quarterly,* Pittsburgh, PA., VIII:1 (1963), pp. 31-35.

were sitting up with him. It was a warm June night and they sat in a room adjoining his. The door into his room was open, and the door opening to the porch was open. They were dozing when just as the clock struck twelve, they were startled by seeing a black animal with sharp eyes and quite a large body and short legs pass in at the open door, pass through their room and into Duryea's room. They heard Duryea cry out in great fear. They rushed into his room, meeting the animal coming out, but Duryea was dead. Ainsley believed that the animal was the devil after old Duryea.*

Demon Possession

At one of the meetings held by Brother Cook, at which I assisted, a remarkable incident occurred that made a deep impression upon the community. The meeting was being held in a schoolhouse and on Monday night I preached when four persons came to the altar, two young men and two young women. It was not long until I perceived that they were not sincere, that they came forward in a spirit of mockery. I allowed no one to speak to them, but kept up the singing for an hour, at the same time punishing them by keeping them on their knees. The next night they met at the home of one of the young people and held a mock revival service, and while engaged in their sacrilegious conduct, the Lord gave them over to be tormented of the devil; they were all thrown into spasms, foamed at the mouth and gnashed their teeth. A doctor was sent for, but he was unable to account for the awful condition they were in and could do nothing, not knowing that the Lord was punishing them for their mockery. Two of them died and the other two remained in a melancholy state of mind the rest of their lives. I believed they were possessed of the devil as persons in the days of Christ were possessed, and that in every age men and women have been under the power of Satan to do as he pleased with them.**

Bad John and the Devil

A man, who was known to everyone as Bad John, became angry at a town of Italian people over some trivial matter. He started home to get some dynamite to blow up the whole town. As Bad John went up a small ravine, he saw an old man standing under a ledge of rocks. It looked like his father, so he walked up to him and said, "Old man, I'm going to pull your beard."

When he pulled it, the old man became red hot. John was so frightened that he ran all the way to his home and fell through the

* McIlyar, J. J., *Autobiography of the Rev. J. J. McIlyar* (Pittsburgh, PA: 1912), pp. 29-30.
** *Ibid.*, p. 90.

door. To his surprise, he saw his father sitting in a chair in the kitchen.

John was sure he had seen the devil, so he decided that he had better not go through with his plans to murder the Italians.*

Slyhoff's Grave

It looks like Richard Slyhoff is losing his battle to evade the Devil on Judgment Day. At least, that's the way it looks to those who believe the legend surrounding the Slyhoff grave located in Polk township on the firetower road.

Every year as hunters gather around their campfires in the hunting lodges of northern Jefferson county the story of Richard Slyhoff's grave is told and retold, handed down from father to son as part of the living legend that grew in the area in which they now hunt.

The story is well worth telling, and we are reprinting the accepted version that was printed on a program for a Masonic picnic held at Clear Creek on August 20, 1936.

The following story, as it appeared on the program, was originally compiled by John Larimer, of Sigel.

It is told that during the 1850's and early 1860's, one Richard Slyhoff lived in the territory surrounding Sigel. He was said to be an ungodly man, having lived far from the straight and narrow, and that his life had been such that the Devil would surely get him when he died.

Slyhoff was familiar with all the country around, and knew about a certain large rock which leaned far over. It is said it leaned at an angle of approximately 45 degrees, and looked as if the slightest tremor of the earth would cause it to fall.

Time passed, and in the fullness of his years, Slyhoff came to the place where he was about to die. Feeling that the end was approaching, he is said to have conceived the idea that if he were buried beneath this leaning rock he would be safe from the Devil when Judgment Day arrived. He reasoned that as the earth trembled and the dead came forth from their graves, the leaning rock would tremble and fall over on his grave, completely and forever burying him from the Devil for all time.

According to his wish, when he died on January 2, 1867 at 43 years of age, he was buried beneath the leaning rock. So far did the rock lean that great inconvenience was experienced by the men who dug his grave. They had to get on their knees under the rock in order to scoop out the earth, and even then, they were constantly bumping their heads. But finally the grave was dug and the coffin placed in it.

---

* Fridley, Lana, "Bad John and the Devil," *West Virginia Folklore,* Fairmont, WV, XIII:1 (1962), pp. 14-15.

In order to get the coffin in its final resting place, it was necessary to slide it under the rock and then let it down with ropes, held by men a short distance away from the rock.

When the grave markers were placed, it was necessary to put the small foot-stone under the rock, presumably at Slyhoff's feet, and the head-stone placed at the outer edge of the rock, with the inscription carved on the side away from the grave.

Now comes the remarkable part of the story.

As the years have passed since Slyhoff was buried in 1867, the rock has moved. Whether by supernatural forces or the forces of nature, no one knows. But the fact remains, and is readily visible, that the rock has drawn steadily away from the grave.

And there ends the story as told in 1936 by John Larimer. A re-examination of the rock recently shows that it has moved even more in the 23 years since the above story was written.

The enormous rock has moved considerably since the day almost 100 years ago when workmen had to get on their knees to dig the grave. In fact, if the rock were to fall today, there would be very little chance of it falling on the Slyhoff grave.

And that's the legend of the Slyhoff grave. The evidence is there for all to see.*

The Devil at the Tavern

About eight miles from Keyser, West Virginia, there is a tavern. It is located on a road that isn't traveled much, in a valley at the foot of a mountain, with a little creek running behind it. The tavern is called the Wagonwheel Inn, and gets its name from the wagonwheel which hangs in front of it. On weekends many people patronize this little tavern.

There is a legend about this tavern that has puzzled many people. It all started three years ago, when a friendly group of people were sitting around, having a few beers. Then came a brief period of silence, in which flames danced in the middle of the room, causing people to become spellbound. Suddenly the devil appeared, and said, "I am waiting for all of you." Then he disappeared as suddenly as he had appeared.

One of the men who had seen him died of a heart attack. The others ran out of the tavern, crying for mercy. All of the group completely reformed. They stopped drinking, smoking, and using foul language — and have kept this up to this day. They also go to church every Sunday.

* "Man Buried Century Ago Is Losing Legendary Battle," *Jefferson Democrat,* Brookville, PA, Dec. 17, 1959.

In the tavern where this happened, the center of the floor now has a low spot. The owners have tried to repair it, but to no avail. This spot may be seen even today.*

The Devil's Wagon

But last and greatest of all the mysteries around the burnt cabin, was the *devil's wagon.* Tradition has it that a hundred years ago hunters and emigrants heard his satanic majesty rolling around on wheels close to where afterwards the burnt cabin was built. One wagoner, who was under the influence of liquor at the time. claimed to have caught a sight of the Emperor of Sulphurdom with his team black as night, and driving swift as the wind. All others claimed to hear, but none professed a sight of the wonderful driver and his swift team. It is said, some seventy-five years ago, the keeper of the Ink's stand, (one mile west of the burnt cabin) one evening heard the rattle of several wagons coming from the burnt cabin, and hurrying in the house, gave orders for supper to be placed on the table, as teams were coming. An hour passed and no teams. He sallied forth on the road to the burnt cabin, but no signs or trace of team or teams could be found. The wagoners told the tavern-keeper that "the devil had fooled him that time." Along the Braddock Road, and down a steep hill to the south, toward the Shepherd's glade, the rattle of his wheels are to be heard, at times, between 2 o'clock, p.m., and 9 o'clock at night.**

The Wizard Clip

This account, found in numerous sources, concerns an event in the life of the Rev. Demetrius Gallitzin, a Russian prince (his mother French) who became a priest, and spent most of his life in Cambria County, PA, traveling over wide areas to found churches. The village of Middleway, (now West) Virginia, where the events occurred, was for years called Cliptown, or Wizard Clip.

During the following year (1797) strange reports were circulated in Conewago concerning a mysterious event in Virginia, and Father Gallitzin was sent to investigate. The story runs that a certain Adam Livingston, by birth a native of Pennsylvania and a Lutheran by faith, had purchased land near Martinsburg, Jefferson County, Virginia. Mr. Livingston was a man of upright character and large hospitality.

* Wilt, Floyd, "The Devil and the Tavern," *West Virginia Folklore,* Fairmont, WV, XIII:1 (1962), p. 14.

** Wiley, S. T., "Legends of Fayette," *Genius of Liberty,* Uniontown, PA, April 28, 1881.

One evening a poor Irishman came to his door, asking for a night's lodging. During the night the man was taken seriously ill and asked his host to get him a priest, but Livingston refused to permit a priest to enter his home. To him a priest was an emissary of the devil. The man died, and directly the Livingston family was subjected to a strange series of misfortunes. Their barn was mysteriously burned, their cattle perished, strange noises were heard in the house, and clothing of the family was torn into pieces or burned, balls of fire rolled over the floors; the family could neither sleep nor find peace in the house. One night Livingston had a strange dream. He thought that he was toiling up a steep mountain side, and when he had at last arrived at the summit, he found a church. Entering, he saw a man in strange vestments standing at the altar, and a voice told him that this man would bring him relief from the preternatural occurrences in his home. He narrated this dream to his wife and neighbors, who told him that the man of his dream was a Catholic priest, and advised him to see one of the missionaries. He eventually spoke of the matter with the McSherry family, who were Catholics, and learned that a priest was to say Mass at Shepherdstown the following Sunday, he went there. When he saw the priest at the altar, he cried out: "This is the very man I saw in my dream." After Mass he interviewed the priest, Father Dennis Cahill, but he laughed at him and told him that his neighbors must have been playing pranks. Moved however by the evident sincerity of Livingston, Father Cahill went to the house and blessed it. For a time the mysterious visitations ceased but returned with renewed torture to the family. When he had investigated the affair, Father Gallitzin determined that the place should be exorcised, and sent for Father Cahill, who in the presence of the family and neighbors, read the solemn form of exorcism. He then celebrated Mass in the house, and the visitations ceased, never to return. The Livingston family embraced the faith and ever afterwards remained faithful to the Church.*

* Garvey Literary Society, eds., *Mariale,* Vol. II (Loretto, PA: 1926), pp. 117-18.

3

Witches and Warlocks

F ew of the literate residents of the Upper Ohio Valley today would admit that they believe in witchcraft in any form. Yet when I wrote a story not many years ago about an unnamed young woman — a well educated, prosperous suburbanite — who admitted she was a witch, I found myself swamped with letters from those who wished to learn from her or avail themselves of her services. Many — about half — of these wanted her help in taking off curses believed to have been placed upon them by malicious practitioners of the craft. For instance, one was a high school coach, whose team would over and over again suffer some bad break or breaks which resulted in their losing games they were expected to win.

The witch, who lived just outside Pittsburgh, was panicked by the stir the story aroused, and declined to answer any of the letters. However, another witch from nearby Ohio who had seen the story, offered to handle the queries, and did so very deftly, sending her replies through the newspaper. Her efforts must have been quite successful, to judge by the letters of thanks. This continued for several years.

Without question, belief in witches in the area in the early period was quite genuine, and continued to be so for many years. In some recorded cases witchcraft even became a matter of court record.

Witchcraft in Court

The annexed report of a case, that came before the Court of Common Pleas in this county (Lawrence County, Ohio), is from the pen of a legal gentleman of high standing. It shows that in our day the belief in *witchcraft* has not entirely vanished.

—————————— ——————————)

vs.

ENOCH H. FLEECE.

Lawrence Common Pleas. Term 1828.
Action on the case, for a false warranty in the sale of a
horse. Plea, general issue.

The plaintiff having proved the sale and warranty, called a witness
to prove the defendant's knowledge of the unsoundness of the horse
at the time of the sale. This witness testified, that both he and defendant lived at Union Furnace, in Lawrence County, and that the latter
was by trade a tanner; that he, witness, knew the horse previous to
the sale to the plaintiff, and before he was owned by defendant, and
was then, and at the time defendant purchased him, in bad health.
He saw him daily employed in defendant's bark mill, and was fast
declining, and when unemployed, *drooping* in his appearance, and
so continued until sold to the plaintiff. Having been present at the
sale, and hearing the warranty, the witness afterwards inquired of
the defendant why he had done so, knowing the horse to be unsound.
He answered by insisting that the horse was in no way *diseased,* or
in unsound *health,* but that the drooping appearance arose from his
being *bewitched,* which he did not call *unsoundness,* and so soon as
they could be got out of the horse he would then be as well as ever.

The defendant further stated, that the same witches which were
in that horse had been in one or two persons, and some cows, in the
same settlement, and could only be driven out by a witch doctor,
living on the head waters of the Little Scioto, in Pike County, or by
burning the animal in which they were found; that this doctor had
some time before been sent for to see a young woman who was in
a *bad way,* and on examination found her bewitched. He soon
expelled them, and also succeeded in ascertaining that an old woman
not far off was the witch going about in that way, and she could be
got rid of only by killing her. At some subsequent time, when the
defendant was from home, his wife sent for witness and others, to
see and find out what was the matter with her cow, in a lot near the
house. They found it frantic, running and pitching at everything which
came near. It was their opinion, after observing it considerably, that
it had the *canine madness.* The defendant, however, returned before
the witness and others left the lot; he inspected the cow with much
attention, and gave it as his opinion that they were mistaken as to
the true cause of her conduct — she was not mad, but bewitched;
the same which has been in the horse had transferred itself to the
cow. By this time the animal, from exhaustion or other cause, had
laid down. The defendant then went into the lot, and requested the
persons present to assist in putting a rope about her horns, and then

make the other end fast to a tree, where he could burn her. They laughed at the man's notion, but finally assisted him, seeing that she remained quiet — still having no belief that he really intended burning her.

This being done, the defendant piled up logs, brush and other things around, and finally over the poor cow, and then set fire to them. The defendant continued to add fuel until she was entirely consumed, and afterwards told the witness he had never seen any creature so *hard to die;* that she continued to moan after most of the flesh had fallen from her bones, and he felt a pity for her, but die she must; that nothing but the witches in her kept her alive so long, and it was his belief that they would be so burnt before getting out, that they never would come back. Night having set in before the burning was finished, the defendant and his family set up to ascertain if the witches could be seen about the pile of embers. Late at night, some one of the family called the defendant to the window — the house being near the place — and pointed to two witches, hopping around, over and across the pile of embers, and now and then seizing a brand and throwing it into the air, and in a short while disappeared. The next morning, on examination, the defendant saw their tracks through the embers in all directions. At a subsequent time, he told the same witness and others, that from that time the witches had wholly disappeared from the neighborhood, and would never return . . . he *had been* very fearful they would torment his family.

The writer found, after the above trial, from a conversation with the defendant, that he had a settled belief in such things, and in the truth of the above statement.*

The Cross Creek Witches

Those who have studied ethnology with the western pioneer as a basis, generally arrived at the conclusion that he was a hard-headed, hard-fisted man, never perplexed by superstition to the degree of recognizing superhuman power in his worldly fellows, and yet there were those who believed in witchcraft in Jefferson County (Ohio) nearly a hundred years ago.

This is hard to realize, the location being so far removed from Salem, and especially so when we know of the sturdy manhood and steadfast religious spirit of the pioneer fathers of the west. They were men and women of steady habits, of iron frame, with resolution that never winced at danger. As a rule they were adherents of the church, and the advanced stage of religion then obtaining of itself would dispute the truth of the statement that there were believers in witchcraft in Jefferson county, if the fact that they did exist were not verified. But whatever the weaknesses of the pioneer father, we owe him a debt that cannot be paid; he was the beginning of the great

65

* Howe, Henry, *Historical Collections of the State of Ohio, etc.,* II, p. 58F.

western empire that we have from him as a heritage. We owe to his memory the enduring monument that is erected in the minds of the sons on the occasions we take opportunity to study the character of the men who blazed the forest and risked their lives for posterity — that their children might enjoy the fruits of their trials and tribulations — homes of peace and plenty. The man who does not appreciate the sterling qualities of the sturdy manhood and unrelenting purpose of the fathers does not deserve recognition of a worthy progeny. The pathway made by the pioneer settlers was a trail of blood, and the very fact that they made settlements at all is evidence enough of the wonderful force of character with which they were endowed; and to say now that they were weak because there were some who believed in witchcraft is to deny them the very factor of the prowess that made achievement possible.

Rev. Joseph Doddridge devotes a chapter of his "Notes" to witchcraft. To the witch was ascribed the tremendous power of inflicting strange and incurable diseases, of destroying cattle by shooting them with hair balls, of inflicting spells and curses on guns and other things, and of changing men into horses, and after bridling and saddling them, riding them at full speed over hill and dale. Of the wizard who was also abroad in this land in the pioneer days, Doddridge says, they were men supposed to possess the same mischievous powers as the witches; but these powers were exercised exclusively to counteract the malevolent influences of the witches of the other sex. The wizard was known as a witch-master who made public confessions of curing the diseases inflicted by the influence of witches. Doddridge says respectable physicians had no greater portion of business in the line of their profession than had many of the wizards in theirs. He says the first German glass blowers in this country drove the witches out of their furnaces by throwing live puppies into them.

In March, 1883, J. M. Rickey, of Cleveland, related to the compiler several cases of witchcraft in Jefferson county, the exact location being on Dry Fork, near where the Cross Creek Presbyterian Church now stands, and the time about 1800. Mr. Rickey's father settled there before the timber was cut, when the stock ran out, having a very large grazing range. Mr. Rickey said that when a boy he heard his father and the neighbors talk of witches and ghosts. Even after he had become a large boy there were believers in witchcraft in the neighborhood where he resided, and that was about seventy years ago. The two witches to which Mr. Rickey referred were characteristic and up to the Salem standard. They were both old women — sharp featured, skinny old dames, who lived in seclusion, and perhaps being in their dotage, gave rise to the belief in the untutored minds among the pioneers that they were witches. The name of one was Mrs. Daugherty[1] and the other Mrs. Armstrong, whose

66

[1] A correction at the end of the volume says the name should be McCauley.

descendants probably yet live in the county. Of course they were not witches, but yet as much so as were the witches who suffered torture in enlightened Salem. It was the same thing in effect, for the people believed them capable of witchcraft.

When anyone in the neighborhood became ill, it was declared that the sickess was occasioned by a spell put upon him in some uncanny way by one of the witches. The people on Cross Creek and also in other parts of the county were serious and sincere in their belief in the supernatural power derived from the devil by old women of the neighborhood. When it was announced that some one was ill through the influence of a witch, the whole community accepted it as truth as pure and unadulterated as the Gospel.

No amount of reasoning could dispel the superstition. The only way to cure the disease inflicted by a witch, according to the prevalent belief, was to send for the witch doctor, William Johnson, who was supposed to possess power to remove the spell, whether the sick be human or brute. Squire Day, a man who stood high in the estimation of the people, as one of good character and intelligence, was a believer in witchcraft.

"I recollect hearing my father, who claimed to be free from the taint of superstition, and who hooted at the very mention of witches," said Mr. Rickey, "tell of a case of alleged witchcraft practiced on him. He had a very valuable cow which took sick, and getting down, could not rise. All the domestic remedies were without effect, and Squire Day and other neighbors announced that the animal was bewitched, and insisted on sending for Johnson to remove the spell. Finally, to satisfy them, and for the fun he might get out of the incident, he agreed to send for Johnson. The witch doctor arrived in the course of time and agreed with Squire Day that the cow was under a witch's spell, and immediately began operations to remove it. He gathered a handful of straw, twisted it into a tight bunch, and after putting salt on it, set fire to it, and after powwowing over the sick animal, said, 'I know the witch and can produce her on the spot.' No one seemed to desire the witch produced and Johnson did not bring her to the sick-bed of the cow; but the cow immediately got up and began eating the straw, which of course was convincing evidence that she had been bewitched and that Johnson was a witch doctor."

Johnson did an extensive business dispelling bewitched stock and his presence was frequently in demand in many parts of the county. He was a smart Irishman and no doubt earned a good living at his profession.

Mrs. Daugherty was killed with a silver bullet. It was the accepted belief that the only way to get rid of witches without contact was to shoot them with silver bullets. Hiram Haynes's family lived in Cross Creek township on a farm adjoining the Rickey place, and several members of his family taking ill, of course it was claimed that they were bewitched. It was then proposed that the witch be destroyed. Johnson having announced Mrs. Daugherty as the one who had put on the spell, one of the Haynes boys cut a silver button off of his grand-father's military coat and made a bullet of it. He drew a picture of Mrs. Daugherty, and, placing it in proper range for a target, got fur-ther ready to slay the witch. Others went to the cabin where Mrs. Daugherty resided, for the purpose of watching the result. The belief was that when a picture of a witch should be penetrated by a silver bullet, the original would fall and either die on the spot or be so crippled that her powers would be gone. Haynes discharged his gun, and being near the cabin the aged woman heard the report, and, ac-cording to the watchers, fell, as if dead, upon the floor of the cabin. After uttering frightful groans, she was revived to consciousness, but not to power. She was placed upon her bed and died in a few days. And the good but deluded pioneers felt that in her death a spirit of great evil had been removed from their midst never more to trouble and vex mankind. The Haynes children recovered, and of course it was thought as the result of the destruction of the life of Mrs. Daugherty.

"Billy" McConnell was a noted character in the regions about McIntyre creek in the early days and was recognized as having power to break the "spell," as the influence of the witch was called.*

Witches and Witch Doctors

There were plenty of witches riding their broomsticks o' nights in Warren County (PA) one hundred years ago. In the long dark hours they used to visit lonely log cabin homes in the wilderness, used to come slipping down the stone-and-mud chimney and put an evil charm on the fire so the smoke wouldn't go up the chimney as it should, and the fire would go out suddenly, and mysteriously. Fires on most hearths, when there were no witches around, burned all winter through, and were never allowed to go out, the heavy beech back-log burning slowly through the night. Sometimes when a fire went out on the hearth it was awkward, maybe the flint and steel wouldn't work to light it again, and somebody would have to tramp five miles through the snow to borrow coals from a neighbor. There is the story of a girl eight years old going eight miles through the woods to bring live coals to kindle the fire for her sick mother. On the way home she was chased by wolves but preserved the precious coals, wood embers, which she managed to keep alight in an iron pail.

So it was serious business having a witch come down the chimney and bewitch the fire. Sometimes a particularly mean, low-down, un-

* Hunter, W. H., "The Pathfinders of Jefferson County," *Ohio Archaeological and Historical Society Publications* (now *Ohio History*) 6 (1900), pp. 285-288.

principled witch would get into a cow and shut off her milk. The only thing to do then was to tie a wool ring around the cow's neck and see that the horseshoe on the barn door was in place. If a witch cast an evil spell on a ewe so that she wouldn't breed, a bit of sheep's wool, burnt on a piece of red hot iron, might start the lambs coming again. Any animal bewitched might be relieved of the evil charm if you could hold it under the water of a running stream. If you held it under long enough, it could be relieved of almost anything. When an owl hooted persistently around a house night after night, it was fair notice that a witch was hovering near.

Where evils exist a beneficent providence always provides a remedy. Where poisonous snakes have their habitat there also grows the herb or plant which will neutralize their venom. Warren County in the early days of the eighteenth century had its witches, it had also its "witch doctors" and "witch killers."

John Meyers, who died in the region of West Spring Creek about the year 1821, was a well known witch killer. He not only drove the witches out, but killed 'em dead. This is how John Meyers, the witch killer, went about his work. A man or woman who was bewitched, came to him for relief. Meyers pinned a sheet of paper against the wall, had his patient stand close to it, set a lighted candle so it would throw a clear shadow of the afflicted on the paper. Then he made a tracing of the shadow and carefully cut out the silhouette with his shears. He then pinned the paper against a heavy pine slab and fired a silver bullet through it from a pistol. The pine slab was used so that the silver bullet might be dug out and salvaged for another shot. It was the real thing and silver bullets were high. Meyers used a very light charge of powder in his witch pistol, it was only necessary to send the bullet through the paper and into the wood.

This treatment was a little expensive but it ended a witch once and for all, killed it dead as a nail. Meyers fees for witch killing were not fixed, he had a sliding scale, and payments made him were in the nature of offerings. They ranged all the way from fifty cents to a fat shoat or a fiddle in good condition for playing.

When a dweller in the Warren County wilderness of 1810 had a long run of bad luck, he didn't give up hope, he knew what to do about it. He didn't blame it on the administration, over production, the stock market or, by any chance, on himself. He knew a witch had put a charm on him and there was just one thing to do about it. He went to one of the fairly numerous witch doctors and had himself switched with a hazel stick. Sometimes these switchings were really severe, leaving plenty of bruises and welts on the patient who wished to be rid of his bad luck. But a bad case called for severe treatment and a cruel means was justified by an end to misfortune.

No one was ever burned at the stake in Warren County for being a witch, but several old women fell under strong suspicion and were believed to "have powers" in the days before the tallow dip had given way to the moulded candle. Numerous old women sold "charms" which would bring a backward lover up to the speaking point, cure warts, cause the object of one's affections to return them with interest, cure whooping cough, make an erring husband stay at home, bring a letter from a distant loved one.*

Moll Derry

Eye of newt and toe of frog,
Wool of bat and tongue of dog — Shakespeare

The most famous witch of the Little World was Moll Derry, or Dell, of whom for half a century many tales were told. Moll did actually live in the mountains east of Pittsburgh, but descriptions of the witch varied from a very small person who rocked herself in a cradle with lengthwise rockers, to a large woman. In one story she is placed under a slightly veiled name, (Moll Wampler) as a helper in the search for the "lost children of the Alleghenies." Her legend was also featured in an old romance, **The White Rocks,** *by Ashbel F. Hill.*

In the following story, "The Erdspiegel," her name is given as "Moll Wampler," perhaps out of concern for the feelings of surviving members (if any) of the Derry family. In it she is represented as trying to help locate the "lost brothers of the Alleghenies," whose fate is still remembered in Bedford County, PA. Her involvement in this search is attested by one county history, which states that "an old conjuror or enchantress" was brought from Somerset County to help in the search.

The brothers, George - seven, and Joseph - three, sons of Samuel and Sussanna Cox, wandered from their mountain home April 24, 1856, and 2000 people from all over the countryside joined in the search at their home in Spruce Hollow. We omit the first part of this version of the story, which is wordy and not particularly interesting, and its doubtful ending, which represents Moll as having been trampled to death by searchers after word spread that the children's bodies had been discovered. Their discovery did not come from Moll's efforts, but in an even stranger way.

A. The Erdspiegel

The attempts to effect an organized movement were in vain, and suddenly came to an end. While the group was in a state of wrangling confusion and commotion, a man, with a conical head and a con-

* Bristow, Arch, *Old Time Tales of Warren County* (Meadville, PA: 1932), pp. 343-346.

ical hat that brought the converging lines of his head to a befitting conical apex, said, with emphasis; "Well, why not git Moll Wampler at wunst?" — an interrogatory which contained a suggestion that was adopted by general acclamation. "Yes; the mountain witch — we mout a thunk of her afore!" "Yes; she kin find 'em in less than no time! — but 'tain't no lookin'-glass she's got — it's an Erdspiegel! — that's w'at's she's got! Yes; I wuz jes waitin' to say git ole Moll with her Erd-spiegel — she's found more childer with that 'ur witch-glass o' hern — I jes tell you — more'n you could shake a stick at!" "Yes; but who knows where she lives?" "I do — I do," cried several. "But who'll git her?" Ah, there was the rub. "You wouldn't ketch me goin' into her den! Why, they say, you can't set y'ur foot down in her cabin without lightin' on a rattlesnake. I calkilate you kin count me out!" said one with cowardice that was brazen-faced. "I wouldn't keer for her an' her rattlesnakes — I would jes go thur an' back in a minute, ef I wuzn't goin' to take communion next Sunday!" said another.

Moll Wampler was a woman about sixty-five years of age, heavy and hunched about the shoulders, and as bald as an egg; the skin of her broad face and round head, tawny-yellow blotched and brown; her eyes small and bright, and brown as a new-born May-beetle; a great hairy mole on her short upper lip; and in her upper jaw two long yellow canine teeth that projected somewhat over her lower lip — great prong-like teeth that, with her round head and hunched form, might suggest, so forcibly to a naturalist, a walrus, that he could not look into her face without seeing the characteristic features of the sea-cow of the arctics. She was known for many miles around as "the witch of the mountains." It was believed she could ride on a broomstick through the air — yet she always hobbled along with a crutch and a cane on the ground; she could cure, with roots and herbs which she alone knew, all diseases — yet her limbs were crooked and stiff and her fingers knobbed and knotted with rheumatism; she had the most unlimited power over the persons and possessions of others — yet she could not straighten her ugly, crooked back, while she lived in absolute destitution in a hovel! But, of all the wonderful things she could do, and those which therefore the popular mind took greediest cognizance of, were the miracles of witchcraft effected by her through the instrumentality of what is known, by its German name in Southwestern Pennsylvania, as an Erespiegel, literally, an earth-mirror. By looking in this mirror, she could see anything in the earth, gold, silver, hidden treasure, or water; and, by an easy extension, anything on the earth, person, house, or tree; and, by further extension, anything in the air, and so on, even to knowing what events have happened and what are to come to pass — in short, simply by looking with her May-beetle eyes into this magical glass, she could see and know everything that it was desirable to see and know — hence, to see the lost children and be able to tell the grief-stricken parents where to find them in this or the next world! And yet, when she was awakened by the knock at the door, her first words were, "Who's there? What do you want?"

Having heard, through the door kept closed between them, his mission explained in detail, and his assent to give her every reward her greed could suggest from long want, and which, the lack of everything on the part of the man with the conical head and hat, could promise freely, the cunning old hag directed him to take the horse and go to a certain place which she indicated, and there remain until, certain necessary incantations and mysterious diabolisms performed, she would come to him.

* * * * * * *

With great solemnity the witch took her crutch, and, muttering mysterious words of magical power, drew a circle around her. Then, observing the dead lynx, she said "blood!" and looked as if her plans were frustrated — as if, indeed, all the witchery of the world had come to an end. She directed the men to bury the carcase under a pile of stones, and exorcised to deepest hell any devil's imp that might be within and antagonistic to her. This done, the blood on the ground was covered with laurel and rhododendron leaves; but even then, the "smell uv it," as she declared, "might cast a red shadow over the glass, an' blur it like," but she would soon see. Then taking something — the wonderful Erdspiegel! — concealed in a rag and secreted on her person — in her bosom! where mortal man would never dare to steal from her the miraculous treasure! — she placed it in the bottom of a black bag. Then, stooping over the bag until her eyes were dripping rheum at the exertion, she at length saw the children! — she declared she did! — when she was looking into a darkness as black as the depth of the bag and obscured vision could make it. Yes; and in order to convince to amazement the most incredulous, she would describe the children just as she saw them, which she did. "I see the childer," she began, "on this hyur mountain . . . they's a-layin on the ground — I see just whur they is — jes whur you be to go to git 'em — they's a-layin right a-side a stone an' a clump ov laurel — they's under a lot of chestnut an' rockoak trees — I dunno if they's alive or sleepin' — they's a-layin' mighty still — I see whur they's been a'chawin' mountain-tea berries — they's a livin', I jedge" — and more such wonderful sights in the depth of that black bag, wherein the mysterious Erdspiegel was placed; that the circle of gapers around her, catching every word she uttered, saw everything as clearly as she had depicted it, — as she had learned the circumstances of the children and their clothing from the man with the conical head and hat, — and lost two hours by so doing; but then, they knew now exactly where the children were, and how they were to go there was all that was to be done!

After a long rest, in which the Erdspiegel was replaced in the rag and locked within its impenetrable safe of loathing, the witch ordered the men to stand in a circle around her at equal distance one from the other; then to turn their backs toward her and each to look at the farthest tree directly in front of him; then to go to that tree and call out the names of the children as many times as he had lips and listen as many times as he had ears; then to look at another tree the farthest in front of him, and go to it, and call and listen according to the number of his lips and ears as before; and in that way, to as many trees one after another as he had fingers on his two hands; then to turn around and go to the right as many trees as he had arms and legs; then to turn to the left and go to as many more trees as he has toes on both feet, calling and listening, of course, at every tree, which would bring him back to the place where she stood, and the children would be found!*

The discovery of the children's bodies was, as we said, more amazing than if it had been effected by old Moll.

On the tenth night following the disappearance of the boys, Jacob Dibert, who lived more than twelve miles away and had not been taking part in the search, had a strange dream. He dreamed that he was walking through a rugged valley by a large stream, and found a dead deer, then a child's shoe. Then at a fork in the creek he saw the boys lying at the foot of an old birch tree which was broken off at the top. When the dream was repeated on the two following nights, he told it to his brother-in-law, Harrison Wysong, who had lived at one time in the area of the search. The dream had been so vivid that Wysong recognized the place from the description, but said it was five or six miles from the Cox home — farther than the boys could have wandered. On Dibert's urging, Wysong took him to the place, first finding the dead deer, then the shoe, and finally the broken tree with the bodies lying at its foot. This was on the fifteenth day of the disappearance. The boys were buried in one coffin, in Mt. Union Cemetery (in the village of Lovely near Blue Knob State Park).

B. Casedy's Murder-Wet Hands

Late in the spring of 1818 or 1819, a pedlar came to Smithfield and stopped at the corner tavern kept by Nace Kyle. The pedlar came from New Jersey, and a man by the name of John Updyke, living close to Smithfield, had come from the same state and recognizing him as an old acquaintance, invited him to go home with him. After a moment's hesitation the pedlar consented and they left together, and

73

* Cowan, Frank, *An American Story Book,* Greensburg, PA 1881, pp. 149, 153-4, 160-1.

a few yards away was joined by Ned Casedy. Passing Updyke's cabin about a mile from Smithfield on the Greenlea farm close to Ruble's mill, they went to Haydentown and took several drinks of whisky. They then started to go to old Mollie Derry's, the fortune teller, to a dance. The pedlar being a stranger did not know the way and instead of going to old Mollie's they took an opposite course in the direction of the Updyke cabin. Close to the cabin the murderous blow must have been struck. The pedlar was never seen again. On the next morning which was Sunday, Robert Brownfield saw the print of a bloody hand on a bar, close up to Updyke's, a trace of blood was followed through Robert Collins, now Jacob Breakiron's, farm to the hill above Weaver's milldam where it was supposed he was thrown into; and Updyke and Casedy were blamed for it.

John Updyke was a low, rather heavy set man and of dark complexion. He gave lame excuses for the pedlar's whereabouts and time of leaving his place.

He nor Casedy were never arrested for it, and some time after he took sick, Valentine Moser (the father of Daniel Moser a highly respectable citizen of George,) had occasion to go to Hannah Clarke's a neighbor of Updyke's and a reputed witch. When Moser entered the house, Hannah called his attention to a picture of John Updyke drawn on the back of the door, a nail was started in the left temple and one in the side. She told Moser that when she drove those nails up to the head Updyke would die, but that she drove them a little every day to torture him a long time. Updyke after a lingering illness died; during his sickness, refusing to sleep at night, unless a light was burning and someone sat by the bedside and held his hand. People said his terrible painful sickness and death was a judgment upon him for killing the pedlar.

Ned Casedy in a few days after the pedlar's disappearance went to old Moll Derry's and asked her if she could not give him something that would put a fellow to sleep. Old Mollie fastened her keen piercing eyes on him and asked him why he came to her for potion when his hands were not yet dry from committing murder. For a moment Casedy quailed beneath her gaze, and then with an oath, turned on his heel and walked rapidly away.*

* S. T. W. (Samuel T. Wiley), "The Black Gang," *Genius of Liberty,* Uniontown, PA, July 14, 1881.

4

Curses

It is probable that one fourth of all adults in the Upper Ohio Valley believe in curses, though most would hesitate to admit it; and a great many — principally among the elderly — suffer either mentally or physically from what they believe are curses. In pioneer days the curse might result in milk refusing to curdle for churning, sickness of animals or persons, trees refusing to bear fruit, or even in death. Today curses are usually evidenced by pain or other illness which the doctor cannot explain or cure, by bad luck — especially in gambling — or by love problems.

The evil eye is still very live in this valley, usually repelled by covertly stretching out the "devil's horns" — the hand closed except for the index and little fingers, so that any evil launched at the defender will come up one finger, turn with the hand, and fly back out the other extended finger, carrying the evil back against the one who sent it.

Curses, in the lore of the valley, are often linked to witchcraft, and to the operations of the Devil — a natural ally of the practitioners of Black Magic.

Trotter's Curse

Reference has been made in this work to the several forts constructed in the crutch formed by the Allegheny and Monongahela rivers at their confluence, namely, the fort, in process of construction, surrendered by Ensign Ward to Contrecoeur; Fort Duquesne, built by the French and blown up upon the approach of Forbes; Fort Pitt, abandoned by order of General Gage in 1772; and Fort Dunmore, the last mentioned, re-christened by Dr. Connelly and occupied first by troops from Virginia and afterward by soldiers of the revolution. There

75

remains another to be noted, Fort La Fayette, constructed in 1792 — and in connection therewith a word about the Haunted Man.

While the army of General Wayne was rendezvousing at the place and time last mentioned, desertions were very frequent, calling loudly for the execution of the orders of Mad Anthony for their prevention. Now, among the deserters was an orderly sergeant, named Trotter, who, in the neighborhood of Hannastown, was captured by three men, Col. Robert Hunter, Capt. William Elliott, and John Horrell, and remanded to the fort. He was sentenced to be shot, and, in despite of the most earnest efforts made for a mitigation or a suspension of his sentence — he being a great favorite in the army, standing high in the estimation of Wayne, and proving conclusively that he was on his way back to the fort when he was taken as a deserter — he was executed accordingly. Before the command to fire was given, however, the condemned man imprecated vengeance from the Almighty upon the heads of his captors, reading the terrible maledictions contained in the 109th psalm to begin with, and concluding with a specific curse for each — variously given by various legends, but in all cases fulfilled to the letter. In the following poem, I give the most familiar of the stories told of Colonel Hunter, who, of the three, was the most notorious in Southwestern Pennsylvania, his fate a terror to the betrayer in many a thrilling and mysterious fireside tale. He died of diabetes in an extraordinary form — of course, in accordance with his curse, that his thirst might never be quenched. And that he lived, from the execution of Trotter to the day of his death, a miserable life, is not to be wondered at: for, bearing in his strange and inexplicable disease for many years the brand of his condemnation to the torments of hell before death, he was spurned by his fellowman without in proportion as he suffered from his disease within. He died in Bairdstown, Westmoreland county, within the recollection of many persons still living who knew him well. The dog at his heels continually is a curious form of a pursuing Nemesis, to say the least of it.

John Horrell resided in Loyalhanna township, Westmoreland county. And that he was possessed with tormenting devils, is a matter of record in the courts — his last will and testament having been contested on the grounds of insanity. According to the legends in vogue among the people, his delusion was distracting to him at times. At midnight, as certainly as midnight came, he seemed to be — or he was thrown out of bed, and held, on his back upon the floor, for a certain time, the while the devil looked over the headboard of the bed at him, his eyes like live coals in the wind, and his teeth in his open jaws like the tines of a harrow! At length he was thrown from a horse and killed, his horse taking fright at the devil who appeared in the form of a white goose that flew across the road, fanning with its wings the fumes of sulphur in the distended nostrils of the animal! This goose was the familiar fiend that haunted Horrell.

Capt. William Elliott resided for a long time in New Alexandria, Westmoreland county; removing thence to Butler county, he died — haunted to the last in various ways. As he was given to drink, it may be presumed that his delusions were those of delirium tremens; for, as I am informed, by the venerable Major Cooper of Saltsburg, (who was an acquaintance of the three haunted men,) he was tormented by the devil generally upon the heels of a spree — the fiend taking the shape of a dog that invariably jumped through the window of his victim!

The variations of this fulfillment of the curse of Sergeant Trotter, like that of Evans, who was executed for murder in Greensburg, half a century ago, declaring his innocence to the last, and imprecating curses upon those who had perjured themselves to bring him to the gallows, would fill a volume.

> *Go where he would, by field or flood,*
> *Or through the glade and glen,*
> *O'er moss and moor and sandy shore,*
> *And then aback again,*
> *Still did he find the dog behind*
> *As when the chase began;*
> *For beyond the curse of the sacred verse,*
> *He was a haunted man.**

The Patterned Earth

This story was told to me by my grandmother, who heard it from her father. She told me that she can still picture her father gathering all of the children around him, close to the open fire place, to tell stories about weird happenings of that day.

* * * * * * *

As the fresh falling snow beat against the window panes, a little old man was busy inside arranging his wares upon his wagon, so that he could get an early start the next morning. The old man, who was a peddlar, was known as old Jenth. Old Jenth wandered around the country every Saturday, to sell his wares. He was a very kind old man who didn't have an enemy in the world. Since he was a hard worker, everyone thought he had money. Old Jenth never spent a dime unless he absolutely had to.

A very strange thing happened to old Jenth the day before. He had received a note, warning him not to go out into the country this week to sell his wares. Naturally he was amazed at the note, but he thought very little about it, since he thought it was a joke of some kind.

* Cowan, Frank, "The Haunted Man," *Revolutionary War Songs and Battle Ballads,* Greensburg, PA, 1879, pp. 110-112.

Early that morning old Jenth started out on his daily journey. He hoped to reach the first farm home by nine o'clock, but before he had gone five miles a strange thing happened. His horses were scared by something and took off running. They upset the wagon, knocking old Jenth off, and he struck his head on the side of a poplar tree, killing him instantly.

Something very strange happened to the ground on which old Jenth lay. It seemed that the grass disappeared from under his body and a pattern, the same size of his body, was made upon the ground.

No one really knows from whom the note came, but it is believed that a witch had put a curse upon old Jenth, since witches were supposedly common at this time.

Every year, on the anniversary of his death, some people say that you can actually hear old Jenth moaning and the pattern in the grass seems to move.*

The Prophet's Curse

Along the southeastern edge of the Buckeye state flows the Ohio River between lofty rugged hills on either side, that in fancy sit and patiently stare across the water at each other, not unlike huge savage beasts waiting to plunge at each other's throats.

Between their huge paws little brooks at last ease through to join the mighty river. Water from the distant rock-ribbed hills, laboriously carried past rocky craigs and ridges, is at last quietly offered as a tribute to this main waterway down to the sea.

Along several of these creeks are places where the stream may meander quite a distance and then return on the opposite side of a sharp ridge of land only a few hundred feet from itself.

The early hunters and settlers very aptly called them oxbows, since in a manner they resembled the shape of that agricultural necessity of primitive farming. The high ridge of land causing the creek to veer was indicated by the backbone, or in the vernacular of local pioneer days they spoke of it as, "the pint."

Yellow Creek, in the early days called "Yaller Crick," was one of these many streams flowing into the Ohio on its western flank, and although a mediocre stream in size, within the last few miles of its serpentine course has had to overcome two of these backbones and formed two beautiful oxbow curves.

Early settlers and hunters always kept an eagle eye for such locations as future sites for water power to turn their much needed saw mills and grist mills. Such was the site where Tunnel Mill was built and where the owner enjoyed a year-round supply of the "white coal" to grind his grist and saw his lumber.

* Thorpe, Harvey, *West Virginia Folklore* (Fairmont, WV, XV, 3 and 4, 1965), pp. 39-40.

It was one early spring day in 1791 that the two young Castleman girls were captured and their uncle killed by Indians on the west bank of the Ohio near the mouth of Croxtons Run. The three red faces responsible for this tragedy were quickly and readily identified as the ruthless Nomantouch, a Wyandot prophet who firmly held to the Indian edict, "no white man north of the Ohio," and his warrior sons Oak and Crow. They were quickly pursued by four active scouts from the Virginia side of the river, headed by an erratic but intrepid woodsman and Indian hunter whose true name was unknown. Because of a crooked finger on his right hand he was known in the settlements as "Old Trigger Finger." His prowess was well known and everyone felt he could outwit the red devils of the forest by his own trickery and cunning. Fear was unknown to him and he never asked one of his fellow scouts to do what he would not willingly do himself; besides, he always seemed to know about what an Indian would do and was there first. These scouts quickly traveled up the east side of the river and crossed over to the mouth of Yellow Creek. They then travelled along its heavily forested south bank to a short distance below this second oxbow and luckily arrived just a short time after the arrival of the old warrior prophet, his sons, and their captives. The wiley old redskin was alert to his danger and so were the scouts. They were now spread out fan shape, one on each hillside, the other following the creek. Suddenly the scouts heard a loud calling sound, so they stopped dead in their tracks and listened. It was the sonorous voice of Nomantouch who had seen some strange movement among the willows down by the creek bank and was giving warning to his sons to prepare for possible danger. He gave this signal to them by repeatedly calling his own name until answer came from both his warrior sons. Then, standing silhouetted on the crest of the backbone like a bronze statue, he silently gazed down the deep-wooded valley to catch a more sure glimpse of any enemy who might be following. Crow was guarding the captive sisters while Oak had started a fire and was making strenuous efforts toward roasting a haunch of freshly-killed venison. They had eaten nothing for nearly three days and were hungry as bears after a long winter's sleep.

As old Trigger Finger was some distance in the lead of his scouts, and having scented the wood smoke through the thick growth of trees and underbrush, he was moving as cautiously as a fox.

The scout and the red prophet did not immediately discover each other but the latter detected some strange movement down the narrow valley and with great agitation and anger was delivering a prophetical curse on this supposed enemy in his eloquent Wyandot tongue. Trigger Finger deciphered him as saying, "Listen! Listen! I, the mighty Winedot prophit, will foriver cast a spill on enyone techin' his foot on this here passel of lan' as long as ther fishes swim in this crick, an' this 'er spill will be on their chillin' frum this day on. Heer et! heer et, Yer cursed pale faces. Nomantouch warns yer to unkiver yore white ears, er die like wolves!'"

When he ceased his harangue and curse his face was purple with anger. He was swinging his head from side to side when at last he caught a glimpse of Trigger Finger. Although then quite a distance apart both instinctively and quickly took shelter behind trees. As the grisly old Wyandot was peering around the edge of his tree the scout's flintlock flashed and the red prophet disappeared. Not knowing whether this was the usual Indian ruse or feint to urge him onward to his own destruction, or whether he had killed him, this fact was to be slowly and warily ascertained. Soon the scouts passed over the backbone but saw nothing of the prophet. They then crossed the creek where they had expected to find the Indian camp and rescue the girls at any cost to themselves.

Crow, who had been working furiously near a large hollow sycamore tree, sprang from behind it and fired, killing one of the scouts. He then dashed away like a frightened deer and was swallowed up in the heavy dark forest.

Trigger Finger immediately followed the direction he thought the Indians and their captives would take but could find no trace or trail of the party. He thoroughly searched the upper part of the valley to its headwaters but could neither find nor see any of the fleeing Wyandots and captives.

Two scouts remained to bury their companion beneath the old hollow sycamore. They strewed the partly-burned fagots over the crude shallow grave. The day was now growing late as they had waited several hours for their leader to return. They rapidly retraced their trail to the river front. Here they found their leader had already crossed to the opposite Virginia shore. The episode was soon forgotten as this was a common frontier occurrence.

Some time afterwards it was whispered in the settlements that silent old Trigger Finger, for some strange reason, had left the Virginia side and had determined to build his future home on Yellow Creek. A few months later some deer hunters noted a rustic cabin in a thick grove of sycamores opposite the backbone and surmised this was his new home. They knew that by the use of his trusty old flintlock he would not be in want for any needed supplies. As he seldom craved the companionship of others they did not seek to press themselves into his presence nor intrude on his wilderness hunting ground.

A few months after the silent cabin dweller had built his shelter he noticed an uncouth-looking person drilling a salt well on the east side of the backbone. He seemingly was successful in his venture for a month later he had several salt pans in operation and already a few anxious buyers were awaiting their much needed supply of salt.

This salt boiler later proved to be a noted character, Tom Burk, as rough as the shell bark hickory when not at his cups, which was not often; and as vicious as a hungry wolf, when taking his brandy straight and frequently. His disfigured nose, ruddy as the brandy he drank and scarred in his many unnecessary personal combats, looked as if it had been gnawed by hungry rats. One ear partly gone, and an eye gouged out by someone ''measuring his eye string'' in a fight, made him as ugly in looks as he was rough in his manners, deeds, and words. Fighting was his special recreation and indulging in hard liquor was its chief cause. The only eye left had a sinister squint, especially so when he would threaten to throw anyone who disagreed with him into the glowing salt furnace.

On several occasions hunters stopped at his salt pans and kindly asked permission to hobble their horses and leave their pack saddles in his care until they returned. He would give them no answer but would deliberately throw their equipment into the roaring furnace and with a satanic scowl threaten the owner with the same ending if he objected in any way.

Salt boiling proved very profitable in spite of old Tom's brazen effontery to all prospective purchases of his now famous Yellow Creek salt.

Many of his callers would question him as to the identity of the silent hunter who lived across the creek in the cabin, but the salt boiler would offer no clue as to his name nor the reason for his hermit style of life. Everyone left some probable explanation that he had been a British spy or American traitor, or even suggested it was love, murder, and also he had been influenced by a witch. One suggested it might be due to a head-wound that had addled the hunter's brain. Old Tom swore he didn't know and cared a mighty sight less.

Some time later John Wells and his wife Mary came and took possession of this backbone, armed with a legal grant for the land issued by the Steubenville land office. They soon built themselves a large, comfortable log cabin to accommodate travelers and, as customary, also conducted a tavern which they called ''The Oxbow Tavern.''

Burk was tolerated at the Oxbow only because no one cared to throw him out when drinking. The usual method of having any peace when he was present was to urge him to imbibe more freely until he became drowsy and crumpled to the tavern floor. They would then roll him to one side where he would find himself the next morning and be ready to go down to his salt pans.

Early one evening in March, after a protracted severe spell of cold weather, a hunter left his saddle-bags in the care of the old one-eyed salt boiler and stealthily slipped out of sight without undue waste of time. Old Burk, with an evil, devilish grin, cast the bags into the red-hot furnace. No sooner had he slammed the door shut than its four sides shot out with a mightly roar towards all points of the compass. The hot brine flew high into the air and all over Burk, besides a liberal

81

quantity of hot embers that scorched his hands and face. In an instant the smell of gunpowder and the sulphurous curses of the proprietor filled the narrow little valley to its brim.

In his rage he swore that if he could lay his lands on this miserable culprit he would consign him to a hotter place than his furnace was ever known to be. He made, as the crow flies, for the tavern in search of this scoundrel, but mainly to quench the fire without and within by drowning his feelings with heavy draughts of red rum frequently repeated.

When he reached the Oxbow Tavern he was so angry that for once he entered without shouting his usual string of fiery curses. Perchance the reason this time was the presence of several strangers whom he eyed savagely with a black, uncanny, diabolical scowl, then slowly asked the tavern keeper, for a gill of brandy which he gulped down quickly. He then turned and listened to catch the trend of conversation.

Mrs. Wells was telling of the unknown cabin dweller and was inquiring if anyone know his name or the reason for his not seeking the companionship of the other nearby settlers. None from the Virginia side of the river could give the information, except one, as Mrs. Wells was certainly much interested. This was his story as told by the guest at the tavern that night.

Some years ago while this scout was in pursuit of Indians who had stolen two sisters and killed their uncle he had returned home to find his wife and children stolen by the Indians and his cabin burned to the ground. The shock, it was supposed, caused him to become disheartened and he left the country.

At this point Burk had emptied his second gill of rum and was shouting about his ill luck, for he was now feeling as hot on the inside as he had lately felt outside. He swung his arms and yelled,

"I'll be flabbergasted ef I don't go up to this 'er old crackbrains shack and drag him down this a'way by his long whiskers, Mary, ef yer give me 'nother snort of red likker jus' like the las' 'cept bigger."

Mrs. Wells, knowing his rough suggestions would be put into action, objected strongly, saying, "Tom, ets purty dark and rainin', an' the crick is gorged jam full er ice. The gorge is jes' 'bout ready ter bust out. Don't go traipsin' up thar, it's jes' takin' yore life en yer own han's for nuthin'. You sartinally hev some orful fool idees."

Burk raised such an uproar that Mary gave him his "red likker" thinking she could change his mind or "fill him to the tavern floor," as she had so often done; but she was surprised to see him striding through the tavern door, mumbling to himself of what he was going to do as he disappeared into the night.

When morning came, Burk had not returned nor was he found in his shack down at the ruins of his salt pans. Mrs. Wells was perplexed and sent her husband down to see, long before it was light. Dawn came, and still the one-eyed salt boiler had failed to return, either to his shack or to the tavern.

Mrs. Wells suggested that as she had heard the thundering of the ice gorge passing down the creek that night they would all walk along the creek bank in search of Burk and also view the damage done by the outgoing noisy gorge. They passed along the probable trail that Burk would follow, all heavily wrapped in winter clothes as it had turned severely cold that same morning. It was the first time that Mary had seen the cabin since she had come to the Yellow Creek wilderness to live at The Oxbow.

The silent cabin dweller had also risen early and was standing outside his cabin wearing a coonskin hat that left very little of his face to be seen. There he stood, tall and trim, first glancing in one direction and then another, not so much interested in the group of newcomers from the tavern as he was by two strange objects, one on either side of the creek. Finally he yelled across to John Wells who also wore a coonskin cap and bearskin coat, saying,

"I'll be gol-derned ef that old sickmore done broke off in las' night storm and that standin' inside the holler stump ez that red varmint, old Nomantouch, all dried up but looking purty nat'ral. This old cuss done stole two purty gals, sisters they wuz, daughters of ole Jake Castleman. I give him er shot of hot lead but the ole cuss has bin standin' thar lookin' at me all this here time. Whoz thet old feller sittin' thar in the ice on yer side of the 'pint'?"

The tavern group walked through the cast-up shore ice to the edge of the creek, and, as expected, there was the frozen body of old Tom Burk. In crossing the gorge that night, as it started to move out, he fell and was drowned and then cast ashore among the ice cakes. The silent man asked if they knew him and John Wells replied, "Ole Tom Burk, the salt biler. Ef you don't keer, my name is Jan' Wells, what is yorn?"

He gave his name, but none could hear it as the grumbling, outgoing ice gorge was still grinding its way past them on its way to the river. Above the noise the cabin dweller called to them saying, "I had a fellar with me by thet name whin we made this ole sarpint skedaddle. Jever hear uv old Nomantouch, Crow an' Oak, an' the fracas after they had stole two gals down the river?"

" 'Zactly! I'm th' 'dentical same man," replied Wells, happy that he was greeting his true and loyal old scout once again and abashed to have lived so close, and to have met him under these circumstances.

Mary shouted across to the cabin dweller who had once tried to save her from the clutch of Nomantouch and his warrior sons: "I'm sartinally glad ter say I wuz one o' them pris'ners — Jake Castleman's gal, Mary. Ole scalawag Oak made me his sqaw. Got plum full er firewater an' tried ter knock me head off with hez tommyhawk, an'

I took fer th' hemlock lak a houn' dawg an' kep' movin' till I got down here in the Yaller Crick districk. I married John Wells, the feller that helped you chase those dodrot criters after stealin' me an' me sister."

"Wall," drawled the new-found friend, "we kinder seem ter all be back heer again today. Ef your name is Wells, an' kinder think yer karect, tell me ef you recolleck what became thet scout thet wuz kilt here under this sickamore tree?"

To this interrogation, Wells with a chuckle, replied, "Berried him right unner whar you built yer cabin, ole scout. He's unnere yore very dern floor."

The heretofore silent man now became interested and came down the creek edge and said, "Wall, I niver wuz afraid of death, but this iz th' furst time I don iver faced et frum three sides. Old Nomantouch don't make a very purty picksure. He sed he wuz a prophit and do yer recollect what he sed 'bout this passel of lan'?"

This made an interesting topic for the group of bystanders as Wells quickly answered, "Me an' Mary both heerd him put his curse on this here spot, an' by tarnation, et looks purty likely et's beginnin' to operate, by crackey."

The little tavern group carried the body of Tom Burk back from the shore ice and the cabin hunter and John Wells later buried him on the "pint." Not handsome in life, his looks were scarcely improved by death. All of the party then crossed the creek to the cabin and, sure enough, there was the easily recognized body of the old Indian prophet standing in the hollow stump of the old broken-off sycamore, just as he appeared the day of the fight when Crow, his son, tucked him there.

The old scout now went with the Wells' to the Oxbow tavern and lived for some time with them, but each day he would visit his cabin. This continued until the warm days of spring. Then he informed them he was going east of the mountains and would never return again. The day to leave soon approached and he made his final trip to his cabin. He told Mrs. Wells that last day that he would leave a note on his cabin door for her to read after he departed.

The old prophet's curse on this parcel of land is strengthened by the circumstances following the departure of the old scout whose true name was never divulged. No one ever owned a deed for this land. The original heirs, the Wells', were both killed during a thunderstorm and left no heirs. Burk's salt works and Yellow Creek salt are not mentioned in a single local history. It was later called Mitchell's salt works and was proud of its school house, post office, church, store, and flour mill, but at present no trace of them remain. Several dwelling houses are now ramshackle buildings that have been converted into sheds and stables, but have nothing in them. The Oxbow Tavern can only be located by the presence of a few broken pieces of pottery and dishware dug up where the garden once was. The post office department gave this locality the name "Holt," but that appears on no map, publication, county deed, or transfer of land. Indians, pioneer scouts, and Revolutionary soldiers have been killed and buried here, but not a grave was ever marked or location known. A vicinity where the schoolmaster taught "readin, ritin, and rithmetick" to sixty-five urchins in its own one-room "buttermilk college" is now passed by a school bus seldom conveying a dozen intellectuals to a distant school.

The Wyandot seer had foretold the truth. When Mrs. Wells read the note on the door it simply said, "No Man Touch." By that name this land is known to this day.*

Anderson's Curse

There have been some shocking accidents at the Big Vein section of the Carolina mine in which many good men have lost their lives. Whenever a serious accident occurred, who in Carolina hasn't heard some old-timer remark, "Anderson's curse is on that mine still!"

It recalls a legend which goes back to the early nineties when Anderson worked at the Big Vein. He was an atheist, and his church-going fellow miners ostracized him — avoided him as if he were a leper. This treatment hurt Anderson and he vowed revenge.

One morning, while walking along the gangway on his way to work, he was halted by the fireboss who warned him that he had detected a feeder of gas in his working place.

"You'll find out whether there is a God or not if you go up there with that open flame," said the pious old fireboss sneeringly.

This stung Anderson and, despite the danger, he strode on. As was to be expected, his lamp set off the gas and he was blown to pieces. His fellow miners gathered his shattered body in a canvas sheet and carried it down to the gangway where they placed it in a mine cart. "Anderson's gone at last!" cried one of the miners. "An Atheist has met his retribution," said another.

Hardly had the latter spoken when a weird, unearthly cry pierced the stillness which petrified all within its hearing. A disembodied voice recognizable as that of Anderson came out of the blackness hissing revenge.

"Anderson is appearing!" yelled one of the men when he found his tongue. He and the others wanted to flee, but they were unable to budge their mule. It struck fire in the roof with its heels. The men concluded that the mule was seeing the ghost. So they unhitched it and quickly brought another mule in its place. But this one was every bit as balky as the other, and so a third mule was tried and it too balked at pulling Anderson's remains. In desperation the men got an old blind

* Schilling, Robert W., *Tales of Yellow Creek;* Gold Seal Publications, Poland, OH 1942, pp. 74-90.

mule and hitched it to the car. Unable to see the ghost, it needed no prodding to drag the car up the slope. When the surface was reached Anderson's remains were transferred to a straw-filled wagon and taken to a little cemetery where the miners buried what was left of Anderson.

Before the sun had set that day, the miners of Big Vein felt the effect of Anderson's revenge. Investigating the extent of the damage caused by the explosion which had killed Anderson, the fireboss found that the vein had caught fire and was now crackling and hissing with a terrible combustion. All the primitive facilities then available for mine fire-fighting were used, but the flames defied all efforts to quench them; water accumulated, the mine was abandoned, and the poor miners were compelled to look elsewhere for a living.

For about twenty years the Big Vein section was deserted. Independent operators lacked the nerve to rest a pick on this accursed ground, even though they had the capital to reopen the mine. A big corporation finally took over the old workings and drained all the water from the section. "This ought to put an end to the nonsense about Anderson's ghost," they said.

The miners of Carolina, however, did not share their optimism, and stayed away from the Big Vein employment office. To convince them that they were wrong, the company had hundreds of rats carried to the bottom and placed in gangways, headings, and breasts and in the deepest recesses of the mine — not a rat remained. Instinctively they found their way to the bottom of the shaft and one by one clambered up its sides.

Unable to obtain the full quota of miners and laborers in Carolina, the company went outside for help. Evidences of Anderson's spell are seen in the fall of timbers, the collapse of countless tons of upper strata, of gas explosions and in at least one disastrous flood, all taking a toll of human life.*

The Curse of Oppaymolleah

There's an old tale they still tell sometimes, back in the hills, to explain some of the features of Pittsburgh's history and thinking. Part of the story is history, too, and the rest folklore, which may be true or false.

The region is under a curse, they say, which has continued for more than 200 years, and may last no one knows how much longer. That's the folklore part of the tale, since it isn't to be found in any history.

It all began on Tuesday, Dec. 17, 1751, according to the account given by Christopher Gist, the man before whom the curse was ut-

* Porter, Mike, "Seven Legends," *West Virginia Folklore,* XVI:1-2, (Fairmont, WV, Fall and Winter, 1965), p. 37f.

tered — if it was. Gist's journal doesn't mention that part of the story. But then, he wouldn't, for he was here to locate land for the Ohio Company of Virginia, which planned a settlement around the forks of the Ohio. And the journal was his report to his employers.

Gist had been picking out some land for himself, too, in what is now Fayette County. He and his young son crossed the Monongahela near Jacobs Ferry, and spent the night near present-day Jefferson, Greene County, at the camp of an Indian "captain" named Oppaymolleah. Gist spelled the name three different ways, and a comparison gives the impression that the accent was on the second syllable, with a secondary one on the "ah."

Present also was another Indian known as Joshua, who spoke English well, was an old friend of the explorer, and greeted him by asking where he was going "so far in the woods."

As they talked during the evening, Oppaymolleah became concerned, and demanded of Gist, "Sir, you say that the king of Great Britain, our father, owns all the land on the other side of this river [the Monongahela] while our brothers, the French, say that the king, their master, owns all the land on this side. Pray, where does the Indian's land lie?"

Gist had no answer, and admitted it.

That much is history. But back in the hills they say that Oppaymolleah was much disturbed at this, and perceiving that the Indians were to be ground to powder between the millstones of the British and French ambitions, he uttered a three-fold curse on the land:

Its gold was to be turned into iron, and its iron into gold.

That its waters would run with blood, and its blood be turned to water.

And that it should never know peace, but always be subject to a vague, unreasoning fear.

For what it may be worth, Joshua was burned in old age as a sorcerer.

Certainly there has been much to make the curse seem probable. More Pittsburgh money has gone into iron and steel than any other product, and more has come out of the same industry. The waters of this area did run with blood,but more often battles have ended or been avoided when one side or the other turned and fled.

And there has been fear: During the Civil War Pittsburgh trembled in constant expectations of being invaded, and since World War II has counted itself as the probable No. 1 target of any bombing attack.

Thus it has been, say the men who tell the legend; and thus it shall be until the time of the Indian's curse shall be fulfilled. But no man knows the day of its fulfillment.*

* Swetman, George, "The Indian's Curse," *The Pittsburgh Press*, April 18, 1965.

The White Deer

John and James Byerly were twin brothers. One day, in mid-winter, while hunting deer on the Laurel Ridge, they separated in order to follow divergent tracks which they saw in the snow. About an hour afterward, John discovered, in a clump of laurel in front of him, what he supposed to be the deer which he pursued. He saw the object indistinctly, but at the short distance he was from it the hunter regarded the centre of it a sure shot. He raised his rifle and looked along the sights, and was about to pull the trigger, when bang! a rifle shot rang through the woods; and John, to his horror, beheld a little cloud of smoke ascend from the clump of bushes into which he was about to shoot! He lowered his rifle, and let down the cock; and, in the sickness that followed the shock which he felt at his narrow escape from slaying his brother, he sank upon the snow. And there he sat until he had recovered from his qualm, when he rose and walked to the spot where his brother had stood in the laurel clump; thence, following his brother's tracks, he continued his way until he came to James pursuing cautiously a bloody trail. James was too excited to observe the pallor of his brother; and John was too grateful to be relieved from the agony of the circumstance, which he alone knew, to pierce his brother's heart with it, so, in silence, he joined in the pursuit with as much zeal as he could summon to his aid. In a little while the brothers found, in a snow bed crimsoned with its dying blood, almost indistinguishable from the snow on which it lay.

Now, neither of the brothers had seen before an albino deer; though both had known from boyhood that rarely such a freak of nature was to be seen on the Allegheny mountains; as they had heard again and again that it was most unlucky to kill a white deer, as James had done in the snow-white doe lying dead at his feet! The surprise of the brothers, however, was paramount to their superstition. James declared that he had not seen it when he shot. He had seen two does together, and had taken aim at the breast of the larger. The conclusion which the brothers came to accordingly, was, that James had missed his mark and struck the white deer, which, unseen in the snow, was one of a group of three does before him. In the excitement of the moment, moreover, neither of them regarded the consequences of the chance shot; as it was, indeed, John was thankful in his heart and James was elated at his strange success. Together they took up the deer and carried it home, and laid it on a bench in the cooper-shop, that the neighbors might see the curiosity before its impairment at the edge of the knife.

"All I got to say, Jim, is, I wouldn't be in your boots for the whole of Ligonier valley — I wouldn't Jim; consarn me, if I would!" said Humphrey Ness, a man of two and thirty, his short-cropped brown mustache quivering on his upper lip like a wriggling caterpillar when tickled with a straw.

"But ain't it a beautiful animal?" asked James, by way of directing his thoughts from superstition to admiration or wonder. "And did you ever see such pink eyes? They are not bloodshot — they were just as pink before it died."

"It don't make no difference, Jim; it'll cost you dear afore you die," said Simon Baker, looping up his pantaloons in front with a hickory string passed through a buttonhole of his coat.

"If somethin' don't happen you, Jim, afore you're a year older, then I don't know nothin' — somethin', Jim — for remember, Jim — somethin'," said Peter Houck, jerking his head downward and a little to one side, with every word, as if lowering a horn before the eyes of James, the point of which terminated in a somethin' which was at least frightful and threatening.

"Yes, Jim, I pity you — 'pon my soul, I do; but it aint no use. I heard tell of a man that shot a white deer west — I pity you, Jim; 'pon my soul, I do; but it aint no use. You might as well — 'pon my soul, I do, Jim," said Harvey Hutchinson, a needy, stoop-shouldered old man, with a chest hollowed like a butter-bowl, who looked at the nails of his toes through the uppers of his shoes while he spoke — until he caught sight of a piece of tobacco lying among the shavings at his feet, when he stepped upon the morsel to secure it when he would not be observed, and broke off his mysterious speech.

And so the ears of James were assailed by the people for miles around; until, at length, after one or two minor mishaps that, at any other time, would not have been noticed, James began to think that he was a man doomed to a succession of accidents and misfortunes that would bring him to an untimely and unhappy grave. And no sooner did he come to this conclusion, and give up care and forethought in despair, than one evil followed another in a sequence that was alarming indeed. His horse, jerking out of the ground the stake to which he was tied, galloped away, and, by some mischance, impaled himself on the stake which he had dragged with him. His cow fell through a hole in the stable floor and was killed. His sheep were scattered and slain by dogs. And, at last, his cooper-shop took fire and burned to the ground. When, in opposition to his brother, the unhappy man sold his little tract of land, at the foot of the Ridge, and moved into another part of the country where his unlucky shot had never been heard of.

With that sympathy, which is so remarkably keen at times between twin children — or, perhaps, it was simply from his having been involved with his brother in everything that had happened from the killing of the white deer to that time, John suffered equally with James, without sharing his apprehension. And during their separation, he was not relieved. On the contrary, his pain became so poignant, that he set out to find his brother, to minister to him in the extremity in which, he was possessed of the thought and the feeling, he would find him. And, at length, in great distress of mind and body, he came upon his brother sick in bed, praying for a speedy termination to the wretched fate which nothing could ease or avert.

"Alas! John," said James, looking with half-closed eyes into the face of his brother, as haggard as his own, "the effect of that unlucky shot will cease only with my life! I don't understand it, but I know it. I am on my deathbed now. And I rejoice that my end is drawing near; for to all on earth, save you, my dear brother, I am more loathsome than if I were a carrion by the wayside — I am accursed! Even Ellen — I gave her the skin of the white deer, you will remember — she has returned my ring. Oh, I would to God that I were dead!"

"Say, rather, my dear brother," responded John, with warmth in his manner, and encouragement in his tones, "say, rather, the effect of that lucky shot — that lucky shot, James, for it saved your life — nay, both our lives! For you must know that, at the instant you fired, my rifle was leveled at you, whom I mistook in the laurel thicket for the deer which I pursued, and my finger trembled with impatience to touch the trigger! Had you not killed the white deer, I would have killed you — and then myself. Aye, my brother, rather bless than curse the shot that saved us both; and thank God that you live — that I am not your slayer, and my own murderer!"

It was the last arrow of John — from the quiver of his heart. But superstition poisoned the barb in its flight, that it might strike with a rattlesnake's fang.

James raised himself on his right arm in the bed, and fixed his eyes on his brother in a stare that seemed to concentrate his existence into conscious agony. Exhausted in a little while, he sank upon his pillow.

"It was the white deer," the dying man muttered, "in the very moment of its death, revenging its slaughter with the hand of a twin brother! It is — done!"

Within the week that followed the burial of James, John was laid in the grave by his side. The death of James not only affected John to prostration of body, but also to feeblenees of mind, in which the last remark of his brother was as constant as recurrent thought could reproduce it — dripping, dripping, dripping, in muttered words in his lips, till the fountain of thought was drained of its last drop:

"It was the white deer, in the moment of its death, revenging its slaughter with the hand of a twin brother! It is — done!"*

* Cowan, Frank, *An American Story Book,* (Greensburg, PA., 1881) pp. 79-83.

Wonder Tales

There are more things in heaven and earth, Horatio,
Than are dreamt of in your philosophy.
— *Shakespeare*

Every area has its mysterious happenings, large and small, and the Upper Ohio Valley perhaps more than its share. Or perhaps its people have dwelt more on such themes than many of other areas.

The Loose Horseshoe

Upper Ohio Valley lore includes one portion of the story of how the family of Anne Hutchinson, the Rhode Island pioneer, was repeatedly warned of impending tragedy by the clicking of a horse's loose shoe. The account here given, related more than fifty years ago by a family member in Baltimore, contains some errors of names and circumstances, but in general is in accord with the recollections of the late Martha Graham Black of near Pittsburgh, granddaughter of the clergyman at Beulah, the church in which she grew up.

In the year 1795, William Graham Mcfarland [William Macfarlane Graham], great-grandfather of Mrs. E., went as a missionary beyond the Ohio river, then the Wild West. His home was in Bloomfield. He left his wife and children behind, but soon news came that he was ill and dying, and his brother went to bring him home. Some weeks later during evening service, while the last prayer was being said, the click of a broken horse-shoe was heard, William Macfarland's wife started from her seat and went to the church door, where she saw, coming up the hill in the moonlight, her husband's riderless horse with his knapsack fastened to the saddle. She fainted and never left her home again, dying herself a few months later.

Next comes Mrs. E's grandfather, a Presbyterian clergyman with a church called "Beulah," near Pittsburgh. On Christmas Eve, 1837, his wife and son were sitting by the fire waiting for him to return from a visit to a dying parishioner. He rode an old horse, and as he was very stout, his family feared that in coming down steep hills, the horse might stumble; but man and horse knew and loved each other, and though he was now seventy, nothing of the kind had happened. He had told his wife he must go to the blacksmith's and have new shoes put on his horse. His wife was talking to her son, when they both heard the click of a broken horse-shoe. They did not know at the time of the part that sound had already played in their family history, but they both ran at once to the door where they saw the horse and an empty saddle. The old man lay dead not far away, having fallen on his head and been instantly killed.*

Death Vision

In the spring of 1846 my father passed away. During his illness, I was with him much of the time, especially in the last two weeks of his life. On Saturday night as I was sitting by his bed, he said, "James, you must go to your appointment tomorrow." I said to him, "Father, I am afraid you will not live until I get back." "Yes, I will," he replied; "you must not think any duty so great that it cannot be discharged, or anything so small that it can be neglected. It is the neglect of small things that causes people to backslide." I remained with him all night, starting early in the morning and rode forty miles to my first appointment, preached three times during the day and got back to my father's bedside at 11 o'clock that night. At 4 o'clock on Monday morning he asked me to sing the old hymn,

> We'll cross the River of Jordan,
> Triumphant, triumphant,
> We'll cross the River of Jordan,
> Triumphant in the Lord.

After I had sung several verses, father said to me, "James, I often thought that to die was a wonderful trial, but I find it a delight." Then turning his eyes upward, his face lighting up with a smile, he added, "Why, there is Jesse Barcus." I told him there was no one in the room; that his sight or mind must be failing. "No, no," he replied, "I see Jesse Barcus, and I will be with him in a few minutes," and in a very short time father was gone.

Now comes the strange coincidence: Jesse Barcus lived two miles from father's and both were warm friends. Barcus had visited father

* Whitney, Anne Weston, and Bullock, Caroline Canfield, eds., *Folklore from Maryland*, (New York: 1925), pp. 195-96.

a few days previous to his death, and on his way home he met with an accident. It was not at the time considered serious, and gave his family no concern; but erysipelas set in, his heart failed and he died a few minutes before father. Of course none of the family knew of Barcus' death, and my father had no knowledge of it only as it was revealed to him as related above.*

A Dead Child that Talked

Now my grandma Berkebile's one baby who was old enough to talk and so on was sick and the doctor said she would die and after about three weeks the parents were setting up with her at night. She died when it was late and the father went and told the other children that their sister had died and then they all went into the room and cried and called her name and screamed until almost dawn when she suddenly woke up and started to talk. She continued to talk for three days and nights and when she didn't talk she screamed. Finally she went to sleep and then no one even touched her and this time she never woke up. Now the family felt that they had called her back from the dead, the screaming being their punishment and though she had moved around when she finally laid down no one touched her.**

The Singing Angels

The angels sang when my mother died. All the town heard it and still talk about it. Della was her name and everyone loved her because she was always doing good things for people. When the people heard she was going to die they lined both sides of the street waiting for Della to die. All of a sudden they heard beautiful music and couldn't understand where it was coming from. Then they saw a light on in a house down the street and thought it must have come from there, but then they saw the owner of the house and she said no it wasn't coming from there. Then someone came out and told them Della was dead. They all said that the music was the most beautiful they had ever heard and were convinced that it was angels singing because Della was such a good woman and was loved by all. The people were Quakers.***

* McIlyar, James J., *The Autobiography of the Rev. James J. McIlyar* (Pittsburgh: 1912), pp. 35-36.

** Keiser, Mrs. William H., "A Dead Child that Talked," *Keystone Folklore Quarterly IX:1,* Pittsburgh, PA (1964), p. 31.

*** Wendle, Mrs. Laura J., "The Singing Angels," *Keystone Folklore Quarterly IX:2,* Pittsburgh, PA (1964), p. 79.

The Disappearing Couple

On the first day of January, 1850, a strange couple landed from a river boat near the mouth of Yellow Creek. It was Joshua Marshall, born near the village of New Somerset, and his wife, a California Indian squaw. Marshall was a lifelong victim of the wanderlust and had rambled extensively for a score of years all over the Western Hemisphere. He had taken a hand in both the Seminole and Mexican Wars, and at last wandered into the territory of California, where in 1848 he was putting in a water mill on old John Sutter's plantation when gold was discovered. All that was known concerning him was that he had married a squaw, and had taken a boat at St. Louis to return to his home in Ohio. When last seen each one was carrying a large valise of considerable weight. The rainy weather on that bleak January afternoon rapidly turned exceedingly cold when this strange couple, with their heavy buffalo skin valises, put their feet on the soil at the Yellow Creek landing, just south of the mouth of that creek.

As it was growing dark when these two travelers came to the old stone house, they saw that it was vacated, so that they entered and stayed for the night. Seemingly, as later investigation showed, they had no means of starting a fire — and when morning came they had disappeared as completely as if the earth had swallowed them, and they were never heard of afterwards.

Some, in order to seek a reasonable solution, suggested that they might have become ill and in their delirium both had fallen into the high water of Hollow Rock and drifted to the river. The episode spread like wild fire all over the Yellow Creek country. The burning question was not so much what mysteriously happened to the Marshalls as what disposition was made of the two valises. Every form of divining wand was brought into severe competition; every inch of the surrounding land was raked with a fine comb and scanned with an eagle eye — but to no avail.*

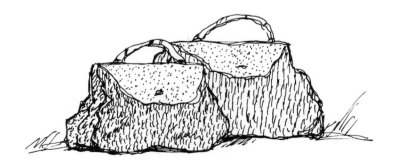

* Schilling, Robert, W., "The Old Stone House on Hollow Rock," *Yellow Creek Stories,* n.p., 1947; pp. 95f.

The Drowned Plane

In the Pittsburgh area Jan. 31, 1956 had been a fairly ordinary day until a few minutes after 4 p.m. The weather was cold, but not excessively so for the season, with high clouds, but clear enough for good flying. Then suddenly a large plane for that day appeared over the Monongahela valley, barely missing the Homestead high level bridge, and plunged into the unfrozen river a little farther downstream. Scores of workers just leaving the Irvin steel plant on a shift change, watched as the plane floated on the current of about five miles an hour. They saw five men climb out of the fuselage and move towards the tail as the front end began to sink. Two of the plane's crew swam to the south bank of the river; another sank to his death and two others were rescued, one by a towboat, the other by the police cruiser; a sixth man apparently went down with the plane.

A fairly ordinary and reasonably successful case of a plane running out of fuel and having to ditch in the river, it appeared. The craft had stayed afloat for perhaps 15 minutes and moved downstream nearly two miles. Dragging was immediately begun where it sank, but given up because of darkness, to be resumed the next day. But when morning came, not a trace of the plane could be found.

The plane was an Air Force B-25 bomber converted for carrying passengers, and was en route from Las Vegas to Washington, D.C. It had stopped at Selfridge Field, Mich., to refuel, and should have been able to reach the capital easily. But about Youngstown, Ohio, the pilot, Maj. William L. Dotson, noticed the fuel was running low, and decided to stop at Allegheny County Airport. Just short of his objective both engines quit, and he took the river rather than risk what might prove a disastrous landing, for the plane or people and other things on the ground.

No trouble was anticipated in retrieving the plane. How can searchers miss a craft 16 feet tall in a river whose usual depth is 18 feet, and was up no more than two feet more that day; a plane as big as a street car, and with a wing spread of 67 feet? But, strangely enough, not a trace could be found.

U. S. District engineers and later Air Force experts combed the river with drags and the most modern sonar and other equipment. They found old concrete, a barge which had been sunk for several years, and an old sternwheeler which sank in 1910. The search went on for years, but not a trace of the plane was found, and now, almost a third of a century later, the mystery is as deep as ever.

There have been several theories. One was that perhaps a towboat had crushed it into the river bottom. But the bottom is fairly hard, and how could the remains have eluded metal detectors? Besides, a tow drags only eight or nine feet, and in 20 feet of water would have left 12 feet of the plane above the hard bottom. Besides, river men felt that if anything had struck the plane, some debris would have been sighted at the Emsworth Dam. The two drowned men's bodies did come up in that area months later, but no debris.

Some thought that perhaps the plane had gone down into one of several deep holes, varying from 35 to 47 feet. But searches by drags, scuba divers and sophisticated equipment found nothing there.

Twelve years earlier, in 1944, a smaller plane had gone down in the Mon, drowning ten soldiers returning from Europe. There was no trouble in fishing it out of the water next day. Then why should a larger plane disappear so completely?

One theory was that the plane was carrying something so secret that Air Force workers had fished it out and spirited it away in the darkness. Some credence was lent by the fact that it was coming from near where atomic testing was being carried on. But how could those who raised it and hauled it away — in only a few hours of darkness, recall — have failed to be seen by workers, residents and travelers in the area? Also, why would government agencies continue fake searches for weeks, months and years just to cover up the fact that there had been something secret? Or sell non-existent salvage rights (an obvious swindle) long afterward? (A seaplane pilot bought the rights for $10.)

Perhaps some day the riddle can be solved. But for almost a third of a century now the river has continued to keep the plane's fate a complete mystery.*

The Murder Swamp

In May of 1952 two men exploring a tiny, unnamed island in the Beaver River near New Castle, came across human bones, buried in a shallow grave in the sand. The grisly remains proved to be the skeleton of a woman, about forty years of age, who apparently had been strangled to death with her own fancy belt a few months before, then decapitated with a sharp knife, and buried.

Officers tried to identify her from the belt and her dental work, but had no success. They weren't surprised, for that has been the pattern of murder in the area for some time.

The island was within a mile and a half of the old New Castle "Murder Swamp," which has remained for thirty years one of the ghastliest mysteries on record, and all within little more than a stone's throw of the Little Giant's now disused New Castle yard. [PA]

It was in the swamp in the 1920s that some boys found another skull. By the time authorities finished digging, they had unearthed seven skeletons. Not one was ever identified, though an effort was made to link the evident murders with the many slayings of the "Mad Butcher of Ringsbury Run" at Cleveland.**

The Rhododendron Bush

The old house still stands, deserted now and beginning to show the age upon it. In its younger days, while old Bill lived, it looked like a little doll house, nestled in its pines and well-kept grounds. Now it can hardly be seen from the road, the growth being heavy, the bushes untrimmed, and the white picket fence has long since decayed away. Haunted by its memories of a lifetime of tragedy and unhappiness, it is part of the past.

Her name was Charity. Old Bill brought her to town from back in the hill country, as a bride, to live in the little house that he had built. Certainly her name belied her character and disposition, for she became known in our neighborhood as a shrew, and it ever became evident that she was not to be tamed, by old Bill or anyone else.

Before their marriage, it was known that she was a devil in her father's house. She was cruel and mean from childhood, selfish and

* George Swetnam.

** Swetnam, George, "Little Giant," Ms., p. 174. (Unpublished history of the Pittsburgh and Lake Erie Railroad, 1954). (Told by an old railroader whose name I have forgotten.)

ambitious to get away from her own family, and it was her own mother who had predicted that she would never find happiness or love in her wild desire and eagerness to be away from all of them.

A short time before her marriage to old Bill, through carelessness and lack of attention, she had caused her father to get his arm caught in a binding machine and it was nearly torn from his body. He died soon after she left home, but she refused to go to his funeral. In fact, she never did return to her home, even when the old folks died one by one.

To this marriage were born two sons and a daughter. The younger boy, Larry, was the only one she seemed to be devoted to, and she seemed to live only for him. The others were made to feel insecure and unwanted.

Through the years this continued, until the day came when the boys went to war. Ted went into the Air Force and Larry went into the Navy. When Larry went away, life became a miserable situation for both the daughter and old Bill.

The war went on and on. The blame was placed on old Bill because he had not been able to stop all wars when he had been a soldier in the first war. On the government, too, blame was placed for starting another war. Also, anyone who happened to be around, was blamed too.

Old Bill loved animals, and he had an old hound dog around the place to keep him company when he was working and taking care of his home, cutting his grass, trimming his trees, painting, and keeping busy. He loved to see things grow, and one day he planted a fine, large rhododendron bush near Charity's bedroom window, where there was a large mound of earth. He was proud of this bush, but it failed to bloom for a long time.

This was the day he made his will. Charity was given all his earthly possessions, but she would have to live there the rest of her life. The making of the will and the planting of the bush caused a great commotion, and it could be heard all over the neighborhood.

This was the time, too, when the daughter was growing into womanhood and was being attracted to the boys. She was a bit wild, too, because her home life was not pleasant, and she stayed away as much as she could.

The day came when word was received of Larry's death. He was in the Pacific at the time. I can well remember the time, as it happened on Mother's Day of that year. Also, I can remember it because a short time later my own brother was killed in an airplane crash while on a patrol mission. This was a bad time in our neighborhood, because so many of our neighbor's sons were away in the war.

Charity went into deep mourning, drawing more and more within herself, and believing it would soon be time for her to die too. She developed numerous illnesses, mostly mental. But she was always believing her end was near. Poor old Bill did all he could for her, but she never showed any kindness to him.

Eventually the war was over and Ted came back home. He had been wounded and was not in very good health. Coming home to Charity and Bill was not very pleasant to him, for he was made to feel that Larry should have come back, instead of him.

Ted soon married and had a son, who was to be the only grandson in the family. Charity cared nothing for either him or Ted, and she continued to be the selfish semi-invalid. When the child was very young, Ted, too, died from the effects of his war wounds.

We had lost trace of the daughter. She was gone, and it was said that she had been turned out of the house by Charity for having an illegitimate child. No one knew what had become of this child.

What had been in old Bill's mind, when he made his will and when he planted that rhododendron bush on the mound of earth? Had he a premonition of what was to come? Did it have some unexplained meaning in their love, or hatred, for each other?

It was now old Bill's turn. He died in the late spring, after having taken care of all his spring chores and doing everything he could to make the bloom come out on the rhododendron bush. It was too late for him, but that year it burst into full bloom, beautiful great blossoms of a most unusual color of red, looking like a blaze of fire.

Charity died in the dead of winter. It will always remain a mystery to us how a large bouquet of rhododendron blooms came to be beside her casket. Also beside her casket stood one lonely mourner, an elderly lady who was the picture of hopeless tragedy and despair, but she had a fleeting smile on her face. We never knew who she was because she left and was never seen again. But some of the old timers said they thought she might have been the forsaken daughter.

In later years, in the process of making the road wider near the rhododendron bush, dirt was scraped away and small bones were found. Could these have been human bones? Or could they just have been the bones of the old hound dog which Charity had despised?

The mystery still shrouds the old house and only the firey (sic) red rhododendron, with its gorgeous blooms in the spring, holds the secret.*

Hunting Friends

Two young men had a lodge not far from Newburg, where they would spend a few days together every year during the deer season.

They were very good friends until a beautiful young woman entered their lives. She was courted by both men, and married one

---

* Weber, Daniel, "The Rhododendron Bush," *West Virginia Folklore* XIII:1 (1962), pp. 6-8.

of them, Tom Ellis. Jealousy sprang up between the men and ended what could have been a life-long friendship.

However, several months after the honeymoon was over, Mrs. Ellis prompted the other man, Jack Clayton, to visit them and resume his friendship with her husband.

Everything worked out fine — and just in time for the next hunting season. The two men, arm in arm, went off together to their old lodge. A few days later, Clayton came out of the woods alone. He said his friend had got lost. A search party went out, but didn't find any trace of Tom Ellis. The State Police thought there was something odd about the whole thing — in view of what had happened between the two men earlier — but they could not prove anything, so the case was dismissed.

The following season Clayton went back to his camp with a new hunting partner. It had been a long trip, and so the first night there, the new man went to bed early. He was jolted awake by Clayton's screaming voice, saying, "Don't do it, Tom! Please don't do it . . ."

Clayton's new hunting partner turned the light on, and found Clayton sprawled on the floor, a hunting knife stuck in his heart, and his face a mask of fright.

The following spring, police found Ellis's body buried not far from camp. Clayton's hunting knife was stuck deep in his heart.

There has never been a definite answer to this case. The people from Preston County let you solve the murder of Jack Clayton to suit yourself.*

The Deserted House

Around the year 1905, construction of a large stone house was begun on Oak Hill, New Brighton. It seemed that this house, from the beginning, was destined for bad luck. And soon it began to happen.

One day a large stone mysteriously fell from the very middle of one of the walls and killed the owner of the house. It was a mystery, for there were stones still in place above and below the place where this one had been. This accident started rumors, which eventually led to the destruction of the house.

After the owner was killed, the house was put up for rent. It was difficult to rent it, because people began to believe that the house was haunted. There would be long lapses of time between each of the twelve times it was rented. Each family that rented the house seemed to have some bad luck. One family was killed in an automobile

* DeBlasio, Alfred, "Hunting Friends," *West Virginia Folklore* XIII:1 (1962), pp. 9-10. (As told to him by Richard Taylor of Preston County.)

accident. Another woman fell down the steps and was killed. Strange noises were said to be heard at times throughout the house. The last family that lived in it had quite a tragic ending. The wife was said to have gone insane because of the rumors about the house. One morning the husband was found hanged to death in the cellar.

Living with this couple was a family of foreign extraction. They fled when the man's body was found.

The house stood empty for many months following this tragedy. Then, one summer, very early in the morning, several mischievous boys entered the house through a side window. A strange screeching noise frightened them and they fled. Later, however, in the brilliance of mid-morning, they re-entered the house and found that the screeching sound had been made when one of them stepped on a pedal of an old pipe organ. The organ, along with all the other furniture, had been left when the last owners fled. The kitchen table was set for breakfast. Moldy bread was on the table and moldy eggs were still in the skillet. Clothes were strewn about the bedroom and the beds were not made. Everything was just as it had been many months ago when the tragedy occurred.

Since the house could not be rented after that, it was torn down and the lot subdivided. Now new houses stand on the old site.

This legend was told to me by my father-in-law who actually saw the breakfast still on the table and the bedroom as it had been left.*

The Dream of a White Horse

My maternal grandmother, George (for George Washington, and nobody could get away with calling her "Georgia") Ann Turner Stafford, was born near Paintsville, in the mountains of Kentucky, and lived to be almost 101. On her 99th birthday she presided at table, and could read fairly large print without glasses. She was a noted midwife, though never charging for the service, and delivered babies all over Johnson County, riding to the homes side-saddle, on her horse.

But one of her more notable faculties was second sight — often being able to know what had happened at a distance, or would come in the future.

A principal example of this occurred when my mother, Flora Stafford Swetnam, was about 15 years of age, when the family, of ten, were eating breakfast. Their house was large, with the kitchen and diningroom in the rear, where you could not see the road, beside Paint Creek, on which my grandfather, Jesse Stafford, had a water mill.

* Black, Esther K., "Legends of Beaver County," *Keystone Folklore Quarterly* VIII:1, Williamsport, PA, pp. 24-25.

On the morning in question someone noted that my grandmother seemed to be troubled, and asked her what was on her mind.

"I'm dreading the bad news," she said. "Last night I dreamed that a man rode up to our house on a white horse, and brought bad news."

My grandfather, who never took much stock in anything supernatural, hooted at the idea, and began to make fun of her. In the neighborhood there was an old man named Bill Collins, a "Hardshell" (Primitive Baptist) preacher when anyone would listen, who believed he saw visions. A classic example and often quoted part of one of his sermons, was:

"My dear friends, and brethren, I come to you this morning because I have had a vision, a vision in a dream that tells me much, and that applies to you, my brethren, to all of you. I dreamt that I went out into the woods to cut me a maul — Ah. And there, in my dream I saw a beautiful grove of hickory trees, every one looking as if it would be just right to use to make a maul — Ah. Yes, brethren, every tree in that grove looked to be perfect — Ah. So, I went up to the nearest tree, but at once I saw that it was unsound — Ah, and would not do for my purpose — Ah. So, I looked at the next tree — Ah, and to my surprise I found that it, too, was unsound and would not do — Ah. And so I looked at all the trees in that grove — Ah, and found not one — Ah, not a single one — Ah, that would do — Ah. For every tree in that grove — Ah — yes, every tree in that grove — Ah, they were all doted at the heart and hollow at the butt, just like you, my dear brethren — Ah."

So, to ridicule what my grandmother had been saying, my grandfather laughed, and said: "Old Bill Collins has had another vision."

"Just wait," said my grandmother. "You'll see."

A few minutes later they heard someone call, for this was in the mountains where you don't come up to a man's door, and risk being shot without asking any questions, but call from the road, and see if anyone will talk to you.

"There's the white horse," said my grandmother when they heard the call. My grandfather went out, and, sure enough, it was a man on a white horse, who had come to tell them that their nephew, Tom Stafford, had been stabbed to death in nearby Magoffin County, in a quarrel over a pint of whiskey.*

Telepathic Message

My friend left that morning while I was asleep in bed, and I never saw him again. Nor did I have any letter from, nor word concerning him, until I believe he sent me a telepathic message about a year after

* George Swetnam

he left Pittsburgh. I had changed my rooming-place to a house about a mile from where he and I had been located, and was sitting before the fire at three o'clock one morning. Suddenly, I thought of him and what he had said to me the morning he left for San Francisco. Possibly his precise words were repeated in my brain; and I could see him in my mind's eye, and hear his voice in my mind's ear — the mind has ears as well as eyes, has it not? — as plainly as though he had been sitting there beside me.

It was then I wrote the poem, "Dust of Years." Next day I read in the papers that my friend[1] had committed suicide in a San Francisco hotel, on the very morning and at the time — longitude considered — that I seemed to hear and see him in my room.*

The Night the Moon Turned Green

A very old woman lived about one mile from the fort. She was considered to be mentally disturbed because for many years she told people that every twenty-three years the moon turned green and death would come to a child of the village.

Since the year finally came that this incident was to take place, the old woman began to repeat the phase (sic), "This is the time of death."

Finally, the night came that she had predicted would be the night of death. At first the people of the village were not the least bit afraid, but then someone said that Tommy Morris was missing.

The search continued into the night, and at twelve midnight the moon disappeared behind a cloud. When it came out again, the shadow it cast was green, and everything was silent.

When the morning came, the boy was found alive, but within twenty feet of the child, the body of the old woman was found.

It was believed that the woman, in order to save the child, gave up her own life to this mysterious night.**

The German Bayonet

Lucas talked continuously about his World War II experiences. However, my young friend was the only one who ever listened to his words, because the older people did not have time to be bothered with the babbling of the mentally unstable war veteran. Through fervent

---

[1] This friend was without question the well-known poet, Richard Realf.

* Scott, Henry Brownfield, *The Lorelei and Other Poems, etc.* (Akron, Ohio, and Pittsburgh: 1910), p. 34.

** Stanley, Penny, "The History and Legends of Prickett's Fort," *West Virginia Folklore* XVI: 3-4 (1966), Fairmont, WV, p. 9.

listening and many conversations my friend derived the entire story concerning the cause of Lucas' illness from the man's nearly senseless prattle.

Lucas was an infantryman fighting in France during World War II and was directly in the heat of the battle on the front lines. One late afternoon while on an advance nearing German lines, Lucas' company was suddenly fired upon by German artillery. As his fellow soldiers simultaneously scattered and stayed close to the ground, Lucas darted for a foxhole he saw nearby. When he jumped into the large hole, he landed squarely on top of an unexpecting German soldier. Although the German was armed with a bayoneted rifle, the foe did not even have an opportunity to raise his weapon for combat. For when Lucas realized the situation in which he was entangled, he dropped his own weapon, immediately leaped from the foxhole, and breathlessly ran until he reached his own group of soldiers. This nightmarish incident started Lucas on a mental downfall and shortly thereafter he suffered a nervous breakdown and was consequently discharged from the service. After he returned home he aimlessly wandered about his farm talking to himself. He always referred to his battle days and forever vowed to someday return to the front, kill the German in the foxhole, and prove to everyone that he was not a coward.

The authorities rejected Lucas' death merely as the unexplainable suicide of an insane man. A neighbor found Lucas in the yard adjoining his farmhouse lying in a freshly dug pit with a war souvenir bayonet buried in his chest.*

The Coquette Dream Well

Companies and individuals tugged and strained to get even the smallest lease Hyde & Egbert would grant. The Keystone, Gettysburg, Kepler, Eagle, Benton, Olive Branch, Laurel Hill, Bird, and Potts wells, not to mention a score of minor note, helped maintain a production that paid the holders of the royalty eight-thousand dollars a day in 1864-5! E. B. Grandin and William C. Hyde, partners of Charles Hyde in a store at Hydetown [PA], A. C. Kepler and Titus Ridgeway obtained a lease of one acre on the west side of the lot, north of the wells already down, subject to *three-quarters* royalty. A bit of romance attaches to the transaction.

Kepler dreamed that an Indian menaced him with bow and arrow. A young lady, considered somewhat coquettish, handed him a rifle and he fired at the dusky foe. The redskin vamoosed and a stream

* Sloan, Pat, "Three of the Tales from Weston," *West Virginia Folklore*, Fairmont, WV, XVI: 1-2 (1965), pp. 42-43.

of oil burst forth. Visiting his brother, who superintended the farm, he recognized the scene of his dream. The lease was secured, on the biggest royalty ever offered. Kepler chose the location and bored the Coquette well. The dream was a nightmare? Wait and see.

Drilling began in the spring of 1864 and the work went merrily on. Each partner would be entitled to one-sixteenth of the oil. Hyde & Ridgeway sold their interest for ten-thousand dollars a few days before the tools reached the sand. This interest Dr. M. C. Egbert, brother of the original purchaser of the farm, next bought at a large advance. He had acquired one-sixth of the property in fee and wished to own the Coquette. Grandin and Kepler declined to sell. The well was finished and did not flow! Tubed and pumped a week, gas checked its workings and the sucker-rods were pulled. Immediately the oil streamed high in the air! Twelve-hundred barrels a day was the gauge at first, settling to steady business for a year at eight hundred. A double row of tanks lined the bank, connected by pipes to load boats in bulk. Oil was "on the jump" and the first cargo of ten-thousand barrels brought ninety-thousand dollars, representing ten days' production! Three months later Grandin and Kepler sold their one-eighth for one-hundred-and-forty-five-thousand dollars, quitting the Coquette with eighty-thousand apiece in their pockets. Kepler was a dreamer whom Joseph might be proud to accept as a chum.*

The Parson's Dream

I had a very singular experience when we were repairing the church, and it is a matter of record in the old book of the church. Over the double doors leading from the vestibule into the lecture-room was a large half-circle sash with no glass in it. I asked the trustees to have glass put in, but they said it was unnecessary since there was so much else that needed to be done. I felt that it should be done, and after my Sunday services were over I went to bed and had a dream. I dreamed that I went down Seventh Street to Liberty and walked up the latter street to Eleventh, where I saw a red lantern hanging at the door of a large building. I went in and found it to be a wholesale liquor house. There were three men sitting in the room and a boy behind the counter. One of the men was receiving money from the other two. I saw them so plainly in my dream that I could describe the color of the hair and the kind of clothes they wore. After the two men were gone I spoke to the gentleman who had received the money and told him that I was a stranger to him, but gave him my name, place of residence and told him what I was doing; that I was a little hard up and thought he might assist me. The gentleman laughed and handed me a five-dollar bill.

---

* McLaurin, J. J., *Sketches in Crude Oil* (Harrisburg, PA: 1898), p. 132f.

All this took place while in my sleep, but I was impressed with it and on Monday morning after I had left the workmen in the church I concluded to look for the red lantern I saw in my dream. I followed the same route I had taken in my sleep and found the place without any difficulty, and on entering the building, which was a liquor store, I found the three men I saw in my dream, two of them paying money to the other man. After the customers had gone out, I told the man all I had seen in my dream and he smiled and handed me a five-dollar bill. I took the money and engaged a glazier to put the glass in for $2.50 and gave the balance to the trustees. I have never tried to give a solution to the circumstances, excepting that the five-dollar bill got on the wrong road, whereas, the Lord intended that it should go to His cause and I was sent to get it.*

Dead Man's Curve

Nearly everyone knows of some spot, place, or area, which has significance for him, either for its pleasant associations or for its sad or tragic memories. Such a place was a certain curve in the course of the West Fork River, near White Rock, WV, where I once lived.

There are four such instances of tragedy, or near tragedy, all of which occurred within a few years while I lived in that area. The first of these concerned a river raft, which was traveling downstream from somewhere above Clarksburg. This raft was made up of logs which had been sawed in the West Virginia lumber country, and which were starting their journey to the Ohio and Mississippi rivers. Traveling on this raft of logs were three Negro men, who had come up from Alabama by boat and train, and who intended to ride the raft downriver to their homeland. Folks living near the river later remembered their sweet, sad voices singing a spiritual, which had been consolation to their ancestors in slavery.

The mention of glory land in their song became instantly prophetic, as the raft reached the curve in the river. It is thought that they may have hit a large rock in the river, since some such jar separated the log raft into its original pieces. All three Negro men were thrown off, possibly disabled in the break-up, and drowned. When their bodies were recovered, no identification could be found, no clue to the names of their relatives, or their exact destination. Finally, a hole was dug near the river bank, and the three men unceremoniously buried in a common grave. A large stone near the spot was henceforth known as the "Blue Rock."

Anyone having occasion to pass by this spot, usually arranged to do so before nightfall. It was said that the spirits of the three men were restless in this strange northern land — lacking Christian burial, even.

106

* McIlyar, James J., *Autobiography* & c. (Pittsburgh, PA: 1912), p. 142f.

My own experience on this same curve occurred during a spring freshet, when the river was swollen greatly as a result of melting accumulations of snow, with spring rains adding to the volume of water, causing the river to leave its banks. It swept with it hundreds of pieces of driftwood, tree limbs, chicken coops, pig pens, fence posts, and whatever else it could dislodge in the bottom lands along the river.

I was coming from the village one evening during a March snowstorm. The large snowflakes blinded me, causing me to lose my footing on the streetcar tracks where I was walking, and carrying the articles I had just bought — a gallon of coal oil, and some shirts, collars, and socks. As I fell and tumbled down the bank, my hat fell off, and was caught in some weeds and burrs, while I continued down into the muddy, swirling water. I fought my way in and out among the limbs and debris, finally scrambled up the bank, and triumphantly caught at the streetcar rail with one hand; but the rail was coated with ice and snow, and my hand slipped off. Backward I went again, down the steep bank into the water, and this time was washed far out from shore into the cold and murky river. Lost, long since, were my collars, socks, and oil can.

"Dear God," I prayed, "I made it the first time, but You're going to have to help me out, this time." And He did.

My brother-in-law had come along in the meantime, and having found my hat in the bushes, surmised that I had fallen into the river, which at that particular spot, and under those flood conditions, was possibly forty feet deep. He had thought it best to wait until morning to inform my parents that I had drowned. When he came to our home the following morning on this sad errand, he found me sitting up in bed, picking the burrs out of my hair. For the next few days it did seem that I might succumb to pneumonia, but once again my life was spared.

Others were not so fortunate. One day, a few years later, a man and his two sons came down to the river bank to fish. After growing restless, one of the boys announced that he was going in swimming. His father advised that the water was too cold, but the boy coaxed and begged, and went in anyway. He soon took cramps and called for help. His older brother jumped in to pull him to shore. It is not known for sure whether he took cramps, or whether the younger boy pulled him down, but at any rate, he too was forced to yell for help. Two men, fixing a fence in a field above this spot, witnessed the father also jumping into the river, to try to save his sons, and the drowning of all three. The river curve had claimed three more victims.

On the opposite side of the stream (that is, opposite from where the streetcar track was), there was a railroad track, running parallel to the river. One day the engine broke loose on this grade, jumped its tracks, and went over the hill toward the river. Just before reaching the water, the engine hit a large rock, and came to a halt, with the front part partially submerged in the water. The shock of hitting the rock, and the shock of the hot engine coming in contact with such a quantity of cold water, caused the engine to burst, throwing off clouds of steam. The fireman managed to escape, but the engineer was badly scalded, and was for many weeks between life and death.

The rock that lay in the path of the runaway engine and which it struck with such force, was none other than the Blue Rock, by the exact spot where the three unknown colored men were buried!*

* "Mr. LCB," as told to Richard Strickler, *West Virginia Folklore* XV: 1 and 2 (Fall-Winter 1964), Fairmont, WV, p. 2ff.

6

Superstitions

T he word *superstition* is currently out of favor among folklorists — largely out of fear that its use (instead of *folk beliefs*) will anger informants among whom such views are being sought. Such a euphemism will not be needed here, however, and might readily hinder complete understanding, since the language has no other word with its exact meaning: "a belief, conception, act or practice resulting from ignorance, unreasoning fear of the unknown . . . trust in magic or chance, or a false conception of causation."

Superstitions are not limited to the ignorant. Those of any area are beyond counting, from those of stock market traders to practices of gardeners. Sneer not at other superstitionists if you have ever crossed your fingers, linked hands after two or more say the same thing at once, thrown spilled salt over your left shoulder or played a hunch on the numbers games.

Because such beliefs, conceptions, actions or practices are so nearly universal, here is only a small sampling of more or less humorous ones commonly in use in certain areas or among members of certain groups more than half a century ago.

Warren County Beliefs

Belief in witches was not difficult to find when the dark, mysterious forests covered most of the hills and valleys; the denser places admitting only a pale, greenish half-light on the brightest day. Half the log cabins had a horseshoe over the door and another horseshoe was kept handy near the open fire, where it might be quickly heated and dropped in the cream on churning day, so that the witches would leave the cream, and the butter appear. Horseshoes were not so common, either, till Warren County began to be pretty well settled, the

109

oxshoe was commoner. But horseshoes were so generally all-around useful as charms for many purposes, like hanging up over a setting hen to keep witches from stealing her eggs, people brought them home with them from towns at a distance often from Pittsburgh or Buffalo, simply for their occult powers.

There is a story of a Pine Grove resident returning from Dunkirk with a set of eight horseshoes for his team. But even freighted with all this cargo of good luck his horse fell, and the man broke his leg. The incident caused a great deal of talk, people wondered how anything could happen to a man with so many horseshoes. Then an old pioneer philosopher, noted for his long beard and great wisdom, pointed out that the man had too much good luck to be lucky, this propounding a paradoxical truth providing food for thought.*

*   *   *   *   *   *   *

An old pack peddler, who tramped the roads regularly between 1860 and 1885, cured warts on the children in homes where he boarded. He proceeded thus: The children were sent out to cut a willow switch. The old peddler cut a notch in the switch for each wart, then told the boys to go and throw it away. A week or so later he would ask the children where they had thrown the switch. Usually they had forgotten. Then he would say, "Look at your warts." They would have disappeared, when the location of the switch was forgotten.

Warts were also cured by stealing a piece of meat and burying it. When the meat decayed the wart was gone. Another method was to steal a dishrag and hide it under a rock, when the rag rotted the warts disappeared.

Eggs carried in a man's hat would hatch roosters. If carried in a woman's hat, hens might be expected. The baby's finger nails must not be cut till he was a year old. They were bitten off. A baby must not be allowed to look in a mirror till a year old. It was considered a sign of death. When you cut a bee tree you must leave a piece of silver on the stump to pay for the honey, otherwise you'd have bad luck.

The signs and omens believed in by early dwellers in Warren County, and some who were not so early, would fill a considerable book. Most of them came from across the sea, a few probably had their origin in wilderness homes, where the wind often made strange sounds in a chimney and the noises of the great forest were all about. It was easy to people the midnight woods with witches, to confuse the cry of a prowling panther with that of some being unknown to man. The far off wail of the wolf pack, that came traveling through the trees and penetrating the cracks of some cabin door, where a guttering candle cast strange shapes in dim corners — was it really

* Bristow, Arch, *Old Time Tales of Warren County* (Meadville, PA: 1932), pp. 342-43.

wolves, or something more dreadful? And then, men who live very close to nature, know certain things, vouchsafed to them through contact with earth and tree and sky, they are things felt rather than seen or heard, but they are none the less real.*

Prediction by Onions

Ann Kelly, a Dutch woman who lived on Holt's Run, in Gilmer County, West Virginia, was known throughout the county for her ability to forecast the weather.

Timbermen of that day, who depended on spring rises in the Little Kanawha River to float their logs and rafts to the sawmills located near Parkersburg, came to her door to learn how much rainfall there would be each month the following year. They governed their purchasing according to her prediction.

Onions were the symbol Ann used in her forecasting — they held the key to the unknown, which she unlocked.

Every New Year's Eve Ann would cut six large Dutch onions in half and place them on a board. Thus there was one piece for each month of the year. After covering the onions with salt, she closed the door and waited until the old year gave way to the new. Then reading clockwise, the accumulated moisture on each onion half foretold the rainfall for one month of the coming year, as well as the time of the month during which the rain would come.

Some onion halves showed little or no moisture, indicating a drought. From others the liquid overflowed onto the board, showing that flood rains were to be expected at that time.

This is a method of forecasting available to us all — at least to try.**

Steamboat Jinxes

Sailors (like many other people) have long tended to be superstitious, and some of the best remembered taboos in the area involve sailing on a Friday, preachers, red-headed women and white horses.

A. The Americus' Last Trip

When we were ready to leave Pittsburgh with the Americus on her first trip, it so happened that we left on a Friday. One of the Pittsburgh papers came out with a long article saying I had taken upon myself the responsibility of ignoring the old sailors' superstition about

---

* *Ibid.*, pp. 346-47.
** Whiting, Clay, "She Knew Her Onions," *Keystone Folklore Quarterly* II:3 (1957), Pittsburgh, PA, p. 79.

the fate of vessels that started on Friday, and went on to say that the keel had been laid on Friday, and she was launched on Friday, had started out on Friday, etc. In April of the following year, while going up the Illinois river, I was sitting in the pilot house talking to the pilot, an eccentric creature named Jack Quick. It was about three o'clock in the afternoon when the pilot said to me, "Captain, they are hailing us up there." The river was flood high and in many places over its banks, and fearing that the hail came from someone in distress I told him to land and see what they wanted. When we got near to the shore the pilot said to me, "Captain, that looks like a white horse and a preacher to come on, and as sure as they are, and we take them on board, the boat will burn up before morning." It proved to be a preacher with a white horse, and three hours after that, when the passengers were at supper, the boat took fire and was totally destroyed. I was at the wheel when the boat ignited, which began in the wash room of the ladies' cabin. I landed the boat and got all off, and no one was hurt.*

B. The Red River Raven

Many who are familiar with the recently popular aphorism about the red-headed girl and the white horse, will be surprised to learn that it is borrowed from the legendry of the river with some modifications. Its origin is somewhat shrouded in mystery, but as early as twenty-five years ago it was a saying among the fresh water mariners in this neighborhood, that a red-headed girl, a parson, and a white horse, were a trio of catastrophes sufficient to sink the stoutest steamboat on the Ohio River. It is said that there are at least two instances on record where the whole three were present with disastrous results, and about one of them a singularly romantic story is told. It involves nothing more nor less than a spectral steamboat, an inland "Flying Dutchman," which at stated periods is heard plowing its way up and down the Red river near its mouth, with its whole ghostly crew on deck, the steam escaping from the pipes, paddle wheels moving, in fact a literal steamboat which once existed and has since come back to haunt the region where it once, like a well-behaved craft, made regular trips for the benefit of the planters and traders along the banks of the old Red.

The Raven, for such is the name of the boat, ran in the New Orleans and Red river trade at certain periods of the year, late in the fifties. It had always been considered a remarkably lucky steamer, and its owner had already coined several times its value from fortunate trips. Her last trip was made in the early fall of 1859. On that occasion a parson and his auburn-haired bride, on their bridal tour, board-

* Batchelor, Charles William, *Incidents of My Life* (Pittsburgh: 1887), p. 72f.

ed the boat at New Orleans, and later the white horse was shipped. The superstition must have existed previous to this time, for there were those among the crew and passengers who predicted a calamity. However, all went well until one night when about fifty miles from the mouth of the river the boat, in making a landing, struck a snag in such a manner as to interfere with the workings of one of the wheels, and at the same time made a frightful opening in the hull through which the water poured in torrents. A scene of the wildest confusion ensued in the midst of which the ill-fated boat pitched once, turned over, and sank with all on board in fifteen feet of water. The parson and his bride probably never discovered what was the matter; at least they were never seen or heard of afterward.

Out of the crew of fourteen men eight escaped by a small boat. The white horse must have wrenched the bonds by which he was secured on the boiler deck, for he was observed swimming away from the wreck in the direction of the bank.

Though this was twenty-eight years ago, there are people in that vicinity who stoutly assert that they have seen the ill-fated steamer on its ghostly wanderings. It is related of one man who tried to board it while in motion, that when near enough to hail, he was drawn on by some irresistible influence. On and on he went clear through the tall white hull which faded away on his approach. In a short time afterward the man became a gibbering idiot and ended his days in an insane asylum. His fate seems to have barred others, equally inquisitive, from making a closer acquaintance with this remarkable boat, and according to the old captain who tells the story, once a year on the anniversary of her wreck, the steamer rises from the river, and pursues her lonely voyage, unmolested. Her course is carefully avoided by the boats now plying in those waters, whose crews . . . think that to meet the Raven afloat would portend some dire disaster.*

"Hayti" Beliefs

The name "Hayti," (pronounced het-eye) without any real reference to the island country of that name, was used until recent years in the Upper Ohio Valley for any early settlement of blacks, whether in Pittsburgh, smaller towns or in rural districts. These are from the area of that name in rural Jefferson County, Ohio.

Closely allied to the strong religious fervor of their natures was their superstition, a trait which they brought from Virginia, and which was enhanced by the belief in necromancy and a species of voodooism

* "The Red River Raven." *Pittsburgh Press,* November 30, 1887.

prevalent at McIntyre long before their arrival. Probably there never existed people who had so strong a belief in supernatural powers controlling ghosts and omens as the African race. This may be in part explained from the fact that like all primitive people their imaginations were easily impressed with any story having for a foundation anything wonderful or mysterious, and their poetic faculty of exaggeration would make each repetition something still more wonderful until finally it would be told in whispering tones and with frightened looks as an act of his satanic majesty.

Before the Hayti colonists had left Virginia there were few families for miles around McIntyre who had not their peculiar signs, omens, and disasters to be avoided by certain incantations and the intervention of a witch doctor. If they believed that a neighbor had too much knowledge of the black art and was using it to the detriment of others, one favorite way of thwarting his designs was to draw his profile on his barn door and shoot a silver bullet through it. Instances of this witchcraft would fill a longer volume than the history of that at Salem.

Many who laugh at the simple-minded negro in the Hayti settlement on McIntyre creek, would be surprised did they know that their ancestors frequently called to their aid the voodoo doctors to make their cows give milk, fatten their pigs, or drive away the gapes from chickens; and it is even said that there are now living in the country descendants of witch doctors who practiced in the long ago. Without Christie's book[1] it is impossible to separate what was on McIntyre before the negro colonists came and what they brought with them, but it did not take the negroes long to fasten on to every ghostly story and every charm against impending evil and make it peculiarly their own. It is a fact that witchcraft was believed in by the early settlers of this country, but that was a long time ago; and yet as late as 1830 the question of witchcraft was discussed by many of the best people in the county. The negro was not only more ready to believe in the supernatural than the pioneers, but was more loth to give up this belief when once it took hold, no matter how absurd it became to the whites after investigation proved it false. Thus the whites would ridicule notions that they themselves once entertained with much zeal, while the negro would cling to them until they became a part of him. It is this characteristic that makes the negro superstitious, and he is blamed for holding beliefs for which the whites are alone responsible.

For a long time no wealth could hire a McIntyre negro to pass Oak Grove school house after night fall, and he approached it in the day time with fear and trembling. They claimed that unearthly lights were often seen flitting about the windows, carried by grinning

[1] A book said to have been written about 1830 by a Dr. Christie, a copy of which the compiler has made fruitless efforts to obtain, giving an account of witchcraft on Cross Creek (in Jefferson County, OH).

skeletons and headless figures clothed in white who had nightly orgies, where during the day the children went to school. They had a mortal terror of caves and old coal banks, thinking them the abodes of evil spirits. They had a curious superstition connected with abandoned coal banks. They claimed that if a man brought his Bible to the front of the coal mine, built a fire and burned it, at the same time adjuring God, performing a certain walk, and repeating aloud a certain sepulchural incantation, old Nick would come out of the bank with horns, forked-tail and breathing sulphurous flames from out his nostrils, and grant any wish — with the simple provision that the mortal soul would be the property of hell when dissolution came.

The negroes would under no circumstances go out of a different door of a house than by that which they entered, saying it would bring bad luck. They would make soft soap and prepare articles of food only when the moon was in a certain phase, plant turnips only on July 25 and cucumbers before daylight with no clothing on other than a shirt, and then walking backward into the house. In churning, if butter did not come as soon as it should, a vexation known to all farmer's wives, they would bind the outside of the churn with a rope of green grass or drop a heated horse shoe into the sour cream. If the butter did not appear after this they were not perplexed by any means, but would find some fault in the manner in which the churn was bound or in the manner by which the horse shoe was heated.

The aged professed to be able to cure any disease to which flesh is heir by means of incantations and by the judicious use of certain herbs, the medical properties of which they alone knew how to extract and apply. Every autumn they would have the roofs of their cabins filled with bunches of herbs and roots which they had the fullest confidence would work wonderful cures. One of their teas had for its chief component part material found about sheep barns, and one of the most efficacious plasters was formed in a large measure of what they put on cucumber vines to drive away bugs and worms. They had fertilizers for the growth of all vegetables, all of them homely and senseless, and they were constantly assuring their neighbors that they would have no luck if they did not use them.*

Rafting Omens and Other Beliefs

A. In Warren County

Few rafts were started down the river on a Friday, though the trip was not hazardous, as a rule it was not easy to get a rafting crew willing to begin the journey to Pittsburgh, on Friday. If the river began

* Hunter, W. H., "The Pathfinders of Jefferson County," *Ohio Archaeological and Historical Society Publications* (now *Ohio History*) 6 (1900), pp. 280-282.

to rise just as the raft was finished, that was a very good sign; a falling river then, was a bad omen. A woman coming on a raft before it was finished was bad luck. Birds alighting on the floating logs and remaining there betokened a good trip down the river and a safe journey home.

Rain the first day of a rafting trip down the river was a good sign, "Bad beginning, good trip," the crew said. If the grubs squeaked much as the long raft went over rough water on riffles, that was a good sign, a "talking raft" was always a good sign.

Out of the bygone generations of Scotch, English, Irish, Swedish settlers, in Warren County, came a strange blending of old beliefs. Trees for fence rails must be cut in the early part of the day and in the light of the moon. When you were planting corn, if you skipped a row, there might be a death in the family. Kill the first snake you saw in the spring and you would win against all your enemies that year.

If you had warts the best thing to do was steal a dishrag and hide it in the stump of a tree. You might then expect the warts to leave. Warts could be wished away by saying certain words and spitting through a loop of string. And then, if you had many warts, you could tie a knot in a string for each one, bury the string under a stone and expect a cure.

To start on a journey and see a white mule was bad luck. Killing a white squirrel or a white deer was worse luck, it meant death. Carrying buckeyes in the pocket kept off rheumatism. Green elderberry leaves carried in the hip pocket prevented chafing in hot weather. A rusty nail in a man's pocket was supposed to aid him in his love affairs.

That some of the old beliefs had an unguessed scientific reason behind them can be demonstrated. The pioneers put a fish in each hill of corn when planting to insure a good crop. Now we know that fertilizers made from fish have peculiar properties suitable to corn. "Lay out in the sun," said the old women, a hundred years ago, "and you'll gain strength quicker after a fever." In later years science has demonstrated the enormous benefits of the sunbath.

Aunt Nancy Range, treating the sick with her own homemade medicines in Warren County, ninety years ago, said to her patients, "You can't be expectin' to keep well without some fresh fruit along through the winter. Let the children have plenty of apples if you can get 'em, apples that ain't cooked." It's not to be wondered at that Aunt Nancy said, "If you can get 'em," there were practically no apples raised in this region ninety years ago. And, when a too steady diet of pork and beans and cooked cornmeal had brought about a condition like scurvy, Aunt Nancy Range knew the virtues of raw potato juice and cured her patients by the use of it. In these wonderful days science is discovering a great many things known to old ladies a long time.*

* Bristow, Arch, *Old Time Tales of Warren County* (Meadville, PA: 1932), p. 359ff.

B. In West Virginia

Working the big raft down the river filled with rage and fury seemed an impossibility to the average logger, but when the man they called "Big Jim" brought his logs to Newport, the worry seemed to cease. If anyone could get his logs to the ports down the river, Jim was the man. Since he would be the head logger, the men seemed eager to follow with their loads of logs.

Jim Miller stood about six feet seven inches tall and weighed about two hundred and seventy pounds. He was reared in the backwoods of Newport and knew the river well.

The day came when the rafts were finished, and the men loaded necessary supplies to make the big trip of twenty three miles downstream. The trip, even though the river was high, would be fairly easy to make — except for the curve called Devil's Bend.

Since so many men had lost their lives while going around this bend, and because they were very superstitious, the men carried wooden crosses on the front of their rafts. They felt that there was some sort of devil who lived in the water of this bend, and that this devil claimed the lives of the men whose rafts did not have a cross on the front. Big Jim laughed at this idea and did not put the wooden cross on his raft.

The first four days went by quickly without any trouble, but they hadn't come to Devil's Bend yet.

On the fifth day of travel, the rafts approached Devil's Bend. The water was swifter and the sound of the current was deafening.

Just as Jim was in the middle of the bend, his raft flooded with water, and he lost his balance. He slipped over board and was swept into the raging water. When the raft which followed his raft came upon the place where he had fallen in, his hand came out of the water and grabbed hold of the cross which was on the front of the raft. The men pulled him aboard and as they did, the water was perfectly still.

Jim explained that when he fell into the water, he saw a man with only one eye. This man, so Jim claimed, spoke to him saying, "You will die!" But as he said these words, the shadow of the cross of the next raft shone on him which made this devil disappear. In his place a light flashed, and the words appeared before Jim saying, "Another chance is yours!"

From that day on Jim never went down the river without a large cross on the front of his raft.*

* Stanley, Penny, "Early History and Legends of Prickett's Fort," *West Virginia Folklore* XVI: 3-4 (Fairmont, WV: 1966), p. 4f.